BRITAIN'S LAST
MECHANICAL SIGNALLING

SALUTE TO THE SEMAPHORE

To Clare

My ever-reliable home signal!

Clare stands beneath up home signal AY50 at Abergavenny on 11 February 2017, as we await a Cardiff-bound train to take us to the Wales vs. England Six Nations rugby match at the Millennium Stadium.

Front cover:
Grand Central's 12.28 from Sunderland to London King's Cross approaches Britain's joint oldest signal box, Norton East, on 18 August 2017, formed of HST power cars 43365/423.

Rear cover:
Northern Rail 142024/150225 head away from Settle Junction and onto the Bentham Line with the 13.16 Leeds to Morecambe service on 1 August 2017, with the Settle & Carlisle line diverging to the right.

LMS Royal Scot 46115 *Scots Guardsman* attracts interest from lineside workers as it storms past England's remotest signal box, Blea Moor, with *The Fellsman* charter service from Lancaster to Carlisle on 1 August 2017.

Shrewsbury Castle and Crewe Junction Signal Box form the backdrop as ATW 158834/820 approach Shrewsbury on 13 May 2017 with the 12.33 to Birmingham International.

BRITAIN'S LAST
MECHANICAL SIGNALLING

SALUTE TO THE SEMAPHORE

GARETH DAVID

PEN & SWORD
TRANSPORT

AN IMPRINT OF PEN & SWORD BOOKS LTD.
YORKSHIRE – PHILADELPHIA

First published in Great Britain in 2019 by
Pen and Sword Transport
An imprint of
Pen & Sword Books Ltd
Yorkshire - Philadelphia

ISBN 978 1 52671 473 2

Typeset by Aura Technology and Software Services, India
Printed and bound in India by Replika Press Pvt. Ltd.

Pen & Sword Books Ltd incorporates the Imprints of Pen & Sword Books Archaeology, Atlas, Aviation, Battleground, Discovery, Family History, History, Maritime, Military, Naval, Politics, Railways, Select, Transport, True Crime, Fiction, Frontline Books, Leo Cooper, Praetorian Press, Seaforth Publishing, Wharncliffe and White Owl.

For a complete list of Pen & Sword titles please contact

PEN & SWORD BOOKS LIMITED
47 Church Street, Barnsley, South Yorkshire, S70 2AS, England
E-mail: enquiries@pen-and-sword.co.uk
Website: www.pen-and-sword.co.uk

or

PEN AND SWORD BOOKS
1950 Lawrence Rd, Havertown, PA 19083, USA
E-mail: Uspen-and-sword@casematepublishers.com
Website: www.penandswordbooks.com

CONTENTS

THE AUTHOR

I developed a life-long interest in railways while growing up in Cheltenham Spa during the 1960s and early 1970s, then moved to London, where I read Modern History at University College (UCL). On graduating in 1979, I trained as a journalist, before joining *The Times* as Stock Market Reporter in early 1982. From there I went on to work on the business section of *The Observer* and later *The Sunday Times*, where I was Deputy City Editor from 1988-90.

A highlight of my subsequent career in public relations consultancy was to support railwayman Ian Yeowart for twelve years in battling to launch 'Open Access' operator Grand Central Railway Company. I now live at Haslemere in Surrey and was a daily commuter to London Waterloo for twenty-five years. I am married to Clare and have four grown-up children. In my spare time, I work as a volunteer booking clerk or buffet car steward on the Mid-Hants Railway (Watercress Line). My first book *Railway Renaissance* was published by Pen & Sword in September 2017.

To learn more, please visit www.railwayworld.net

INTRODUCTION

By rights, it should have disappeared decades ago. Mechanical signalling, with its distinctive swish of signal wires being pulled and that satisfying clunk as a signal arm is raised or lowered, has been on the way out for almost 80 years. Colour light signals were introduced during the pre-grouping era in the early-1920s, yet here we are today with a number of significant stretches of line reliant on Victorian technology to control the safety of our railway network.

There is, of course, a masterplan in place which will finally spell the end of mechanical signal boxes and the semaphore signals which a good many of them still control. This is the Network Rail plan to migrate all control to a dozen or so Railway Operating Centres (ROCs), with a timetable stretching forward to around 2050 for the elimination of the last vestiges of local signalling control.

But things don't always run to timetable on the railways, as any daily commuter will attest. There has already been significant slippage to the published plans for signalling replacement and talking to signallers in various parts of the country it looks like many of the published targets may slip further still, so the end may not quite be nigh for the much-loved semaphore signal. Indeed, an update from Network Rail has confirmed to me that there will still be more than 1,200 semaphore signals on the network by the end of what is known as Control Period 6 in April 2024.

Steam meets semaphore at Fort William where K1 locomotive 62005 heads The Jacobite service to Mallaig on 5 October 2017 and approaches signal FW25, from which point onwards, the route is controlled by radio signalling.

DB 66129 passes the most celebrated surviving signal on the entire British rail network, the Midland Railway lower quadrant at Ketton, near Stamford. It is hauling an aggregates train from Mountsorrel to Trowse Yard, Norwich, on 28 September 2017.

Widespread replacement of semaphore signalling has been taking place since the 1960s and the programme continues. Relatively recent losses include the routes from Ely to Norwich, where many of the fine signal boxes are listed structures which remain in place some years after their functions were lost in 2012 to a control centre at Cambridge. Other significant recent disappearances are the Mid-Sussex line from Pulborough to Barnham and the line through Barnetby in Lincolnshire, which boasted some of the finest remaining semaphore signals until replacement in December 2015.

In addition to these, a number of locations featured in this book and visited during 2016 and 2017 will have seen their semaphores eliminated by the time these words and pictures are published. Notable amongst these will be in the north of Scotland at Forres and Elgin, where a £135 million upgrade of the Inverness to Aberdeen route includes a re-siting of Forres station, the Blackpool North to Preston route, which has been both re-signalled and electrified and, on the banks of the Humber, the fascinating ten-mile stretch of line from Gilberdyke Junction to Melton Lane, between Brough and Ferriby.

Elsewhere, the £50 million North Wales Railway Upgrade Project, completed on schedule in Spring 2018, saw elimination of semaphore signalling at a trio of locations and historic signal boxes featured

in this book – Prestatyn, Abergele & Pensarn and Rhyl – while a bitter blow for lovers of traditional signalling in 2019 will be replacement of mechanical signalling on the delightful Wherry Lines from Norwich to Great Yarmouth and Lowestoft.

In addition to these losses, other places to have lost the semaphores featured in these pages include Pitlochry and Aviemore on the Highland Main Line in Scotland, Newhaven Harbour in East Sussex, Frodsham in the north-west and Craven Arms on the Marches Line, where re-siting of a cross-over used by Heart of Wales Line trains to a point south of the station will mean removal of a number of semaphore arms.

My inspiration for this book came when travelling the country to sample revived and re-opened lines for my first book, *Railway Renaissance*. In doing so, I realised that capturing images which featured semaphore signals gave a sense of context and history to what I was photographing and so grew the germ of an idea to move my focus away from the lines and trains themselves and to capture as much as possible of our remarkable signalling heritage.

While many fine signal boxes remain, only a small proportion of them still control semaphore signals and, in many cases, only a handful of signals apiece. In the case of the South of England, for example (Chapter Two) there are no remaining routes where semaphore signals remain, apart from the short, inaccessible and freight-only Dudding Hill Line in North London, but there are isolated survivors in places as far afield as Greenford in North-West London, Deal in Kent, the seaside resorts of Hastings, Bognor Regis and Littlehampton on the South Coast and Yeovil in Somerset.

Nevertheless, at the time of writing there are still sections of route across the remainder of England, as well as in Scotland and in Wales, where there are significant outposts of mechanical signalling to be viewed and appreciated. As the following chapters will hopefully

Blackpool Tower dominates the sky-line as Northern Rail 156491/428 are signalled out of platform 6 at Blackpool North station on 22 September 2017 with the 10.40 to Manchester Airport.

bring to life, there are fine examples in Cornwall (seven mechanical boxes between Liskeard to St. Erth), while other notable survivals are in East Anglia (nine boxes with mechanical signalling on the Wherry lines from Norwich to Great Yarmouth and Lowestoft) and the Marches Line northwards from Newport to Shrewsbury where there are a dozen surviving boxes from Little Mill Junction near Abergavenny to the 'big daddy' of mechanical signalling, Severn Bridge Junction at Shrewsbury.

Elsewhere, routes and locations to particularly savour range from Moreton-in-Marsh via Worcester to Ledbury on the Cotswold Line (eight boxes with mechanical signalling, plus two others in the Worcester area), the famous Settle to Carlisle Line, the Cumbrian Coast line and, in the East Midlands, the Poacher Line from Grantham to Skegness, as well as a number of locations in the North-East, notably the oldest surviving boxes of all at Norton South and Norton East near Stockton-on-Tees.

Scotland also remains well blessed with mechanical signalling. While the two listed signal boxes at Stirling have lost all their once fine array of historic semaphores, head north up the Highland Line and there are a fascinating collection of signal boxes, every one different, as well as historic Highland Railway lattice post semaphores at places including Dunkeld and Blair Atholl.

North-East Scotland, too, retains a good number of semaphore signals between Inverness, Aberdeen and Dundee. At the opposite end of the country, semaphores survive at a number of places along the Glasgow to Kilmarnock and Carlisle route, while a 40-mile stretch of line from Girvan to Stranraer Harbour not only boasts five mechanical signal boxes

Northern Rail 158843 has just left Gilberdyke station on 9 August 2017 and approaches the signal box and junction with the 10.31 Hull-York service.

(although Stranraer Harbour has long been 'switched out'), but also represents the last section of line in the whole of Great Britain to be controlled by large circular Victorian Tyer's tablets, a larger form of the tokens used elsewhere.

Across the Irish Sea, a similar process of centralizing signal control is also underway. Yet here, too, there are a few remaining manual signal boxes controlling the distinctive and almost fluorescent orange-coloured and lower quadrant semaphore arms along two of the Republic's most loss-making and endangered railway routes – Limerick to Ballybrophy and Limerick Junction to Waterford. Elsewhere, manual signalling has been replaced at Limerick and Cork since my January 2017 visit, but isolated examples remain - as featured in Chapter Nine.

The focus of this book is primarily on working semaphore signals controlling passenger and freight running lines, but there are other examples of mechanical signalling to note. These are the short-armed shunting signals and discs, which in some cases have survived when all other signals in the vicinity have been replaced by colour lights. Examples noted in the following chapters include March and Sleaford, but others worthy

British signalling expertise was exported across the empire and some of it survives to this day, notably in Sri Lanka, where the finest signals of all can be found in Kandy. Seen here on 11 July 2017 is its famous signal gantry, with the signal box behind, home to a 63-lever Saxby & Farmer lever frame.

of mention include those in the goods yard at Peterborough, which can be seen from trains passing on the East Coast Main Line and are controlled by Eastfield signal box, while there are others in the yards at Willesden Junction and Tyseley, and manually-worked shunt signals at Wokingham, for example.

Travelling the length and breadth of Great Britain, it has been interesting to note that a significant number of semaphore signals appear relatively modern, notably those mounted on rectangular galvanised steel posts. There are examples, too, where semaphores have been installed in recent years – at Moreton-in-Marsh in 2011, at Malvern Wells in 2016 and at Gainsborough Central and Henwick in 2017. According to Network Rail, factors in deciding when

a new or replacement semaphore signal would be installed, rather than a colour light, include the question of how long it is likely to be until the particular area is due to be re-signalled, and thus whether a like-for-like replacement is financially advantageous.

A brief history of mechanical signalling

What remains of mechanical signalling today has its origins in the 1860s, when the interlocked signal box was first developed, and then expanded across Britain during the 1870s and 1880s, from which era the network's oldest signal boxes date. The oldest surviving mechanical signal box in daily use is Norton South, near Stockton-on-Tees, which dates from 1870, along with

No weed-killing train has been down the Newquay branch for some time, to judge by the state of the track at St. Blazey which XC 220005 approaches on 24 June 2017 with the 15.30 Newquay-Manchester Piccadilly.

nearby Norton East, although the latter remains largely 'switched out'.

Other very early examples still in use, and featured in this book, are Bootle (1871), Ty Croes, Heighington, Marsh Brook, North Seaton, Prudhoe and Tutbury Crossing (all 1872); Ancaster, Bromfield, Hilton Junction, Howsham, Knaresborough and Weaverthorpe (all 1873), Bardon Mill, Barnhill, Gristhorpe and West Street Junction, Boston (all 1874).

Development of interlocked signalling was a crucial development in railway safety, by making it physically impossible to operate signal and points levers in the wrong sequence, so that a signal could only be pulled into the 'off' position if a set of points ahead of it had been correctly set. The first attempt at interlocked signals and points was at Bricklayers Arms Junction, in South-East London in 1856, which was the work of a notable signalling pioneer called John Saxby, but it was four years later, in 1860, that Kentish Town Junction became

the first fully interlocked lever frame to control both signals and related points.

Saxby had worked as a carpenter on the London, Brighton & South Coast Railway (LBSCR) during the 1850s and had secured a patent on the system of interlocking introduced at Bricklayers Arms in 1856. He teamed up with another LBSCR man, John Farmer, to found what was to become Britain's pre-eminent firm of signalling engineers, Saxby & Farmer, many of whose lever frames remain in use in signal boxes in Great Britain and overseas to this day.

In parallel with the development of interlocking in the 1860s, along with the first signal boxes came another crucial development in rail safety, known as the Block System. This was an electronic means of communicating between signal boxes to ensure that only one train could be on a stretch of track between two signal boxes at any one time, with the section of track known as the Block and the system itself called Absolute Block.

ATW 175105 accelerates away from Helsby on 10 June 2017 with the 13.33 Bangor-Manchester Airport service.

Despite the reluctance of some railway companies, a number of major accidents, notably one at Clayton Tunnel on the Brighton main line in August 1861, meant the Block System soon replaced the earlier time interval method of separating trains. It finally became compulsory under the terms of the 1889 Regulation of Railways Act, which was passed by parliament in the wake of another major crash, at Armagh in Northern Ireland on 12 June 1889, where 78 passengers on an excursion train were killed, 22 of them children, when the brakes on part of a train they were travelling in failed, and it was hit by a proceeding train which was operating under normal time interval rules.

Another major nineteenth century development in British signalling was track circuits, the running of an electric current through the rails themselves to detect the presence of a train on a section of line. This in turn led to the ability to introduce automatic signals, and what is known as Track Circuit Block signalling, by which the Block became the space between the signals, rather than simply the section of line between two signal boxes.

The workings of semaphore signalling

There are two types of semaphore signalling arm, the red home or stop signal with a white stripe near one end and the yellow distant arm, with its distinctive fishtail end and a black stripe. Many are mounted on separate signal posts, but in areas where the signal boxes are close together, such as on a main line, a single post will have a home signal mounted above a distant, with the latter worked from the following signal box and inter-locked in such a way that the distant can only be pulled into the 'off' position once the home signal above is 'off'.

Semaphore signals come in two distinct forms, upper and lower quadrant. In the early days of mechanical signalling, lower quadrant was adopted as the standard that is a signal arm which would be at

The line from Girvan to Stranraer in south west Scotland is the last in Britain to be controlled by the Tyer's Tablet. Seen here is a tablet for the Glenwhilly-Dunragit section of this scenic route.

45 degrees below the horizontal to indicate 'line clear'. There were concerns, however, that in the event of a signal wire breaking the arm would fall to the 'line clear' position, with potentially catastrophic consequences, so from the 1920s, these lower quadrant signals were largely replaced by upper quadrant signals, which were deemed safer, since any wire failure when a signal was in the 'off' (45 degrees above the horizontal) position would simply see the arm fall to the horizontal 'stop' position.

The one exception to this standard practice was on lines of the former Great Western Railway, which boasted an exemplary safety record and stuck with lower quadrant signals. Today lower quadrant signals survive on sections of the former GWR, notably in Cornwall and on the Marches Line from Shrewsbury to Abergavenny, while virtually all other remaining semaphore signals in Britain are of the upper quadrant type, two exceptions being an historic Midland Railway signal at Ketton and the last surviving 'somersault' signal at Boston Docks, both featured elsewhere in this story. There are even places with both upper and lower quadrant signals, such as Gobowen, Shrewsbury and Yeovil Pen Mill.

Besides the moving arm, a semaphore signal also comprises what is known as a spectacle, a pair of coloured lenses at the post-end of the signal arm, which are illuminated by a lamp and, in the case of a stop (home) signal, will show a red aspect when the signal is at danger and a green

Somersault signals were once a feature of many routes in eastern England. Today the only remaining example is this one on the Boston Docks branch in Lincolnshire, seen here on 30 March 2017 shortly before a train of steel coil emerged from the docks.

Working distant signals are sometimes difficult to access, but one with a good vantage point is the Reedham Junction up distant (RJ60), seen here on 17 March 2017 as DRS-owned 68003/016 pass with the 14.57 Lowestoft-Norwich service.

when it is in the off position. In the case of a distant signal, the top spectacle will be yellow, to show a caution warning to the driver, with a green aspect below (in the case of a lower quadrant signal) or above, in the case of an upper quadrant distant. Where there are issues of visibility, a white 'sighting board' may be positioned behind the signal arm, while in some cases a white square will be painted onto a nearby over-bridge, for the same purpose.

Positioning semaphore signals would vary between locations, but there are certain standard characteristics. The closest stop signals on each side of a signal box (approaching the box) are known as its home signals. These may be termed inner home if there is another stop signal further back down the line, which would then be known as the outer home; to confuse matters ever more there might also be an intermediate home between these two signals.

Furthest from the box in the direction a train was approaching from would be the distant signal, up to a mile from the box

and sometimes motor-operated. Having passed a signal box, the first signal beyond will be a starter (often located at or close to a platform end), after which would come an advanced starter, which is often referred to by signallers as the 'section signal' as it controls access to the next section or block.

A long-running programme of replacement

Colour light signals have been a feature of the British railway scene since the 1920s, but the wholesale programme of replacing mechanical (semaphore) signalling only began in earnest in the 1960s. The concept of three and four aspect colour light signals was agreed by the Institute of Railway Signal Engineers in 1924 and the first such signals were installed by the Southern Railway just two years later, in 1926.

While most railway companies adopted three and four aspect lights, an

alternative used in a number of places, including East Anglia, were what are known as searchlight signals, with just one light and a moving glass aspect that would allow it to change from red to amber and green. These searchlight signals fell out of favour in about 1960, but are very similar in appearance to the new single aspect LED signals now being adopted, although in this case, the change in colour is achieved through having a multi-coloured cluster of LED lights, rather than the movement of a multi-coloured lens in front of the light.

At its peak in the early 1900s, the British railway network boasted an estimated 12,000 to 13,000 signal boxes, but that number began to decline as railway companies in the 1920s and 1930s began to rationalise in places where stations had two or more boxes. That process accelerated with the 1955 Modernisation Plan for British Railways and the subsequent decade of line closures

following publication of the infamous 'Beeching Report' in 1963.

By 1970, the number of signal boxes in Great Britain had shrunk to around 4,000 and that process has continued to a current situation where we have around 500 signal boxes on the network of which, at the start of 2015, 373 were mechanical signal boxes, according to a Network Rail response to a 'Freedom of Information Act' request. That number has since been further reduced to a September 2017 total of 337 boxes, according to data supplied to me by Network Rail, through continued re-signalling programmes.

The 2015 figure also included boxes where no semaphore signals remained but, according to my analysis of that list, there remained (as of October 2017) approximately 200 locations across Great Britain where there are signal boxes controlling at least one semaphore, the great majority of these locations being featured in this book.

One of many fine and listed signal boxes in Scotland is Arbroath North, a North British Railway design from 1911. It was designed specifically for this location with additional height and is the country's only box with an over-sailing signal cabin supported on metal brackets projecting toward the track.

Railway Operating Centres (ROC)

Under the masterplan currently being implemented by Network Rail, all existing signal boxes, not just those mechanical ones featured in this book, will be replaced by a small number of Railway Operating Centres (ROCs), as well as a number of other centralised control points. According to the information supplied to me by Network Rail for this book, confirmed locations for seven ROCs are Basingstoke (Wessex), Three Bridges (South-East and Sussex), York (London and North Eastern), Rugby (London and North Western south), Manchester (London and North Western north), Romford (Anglia) and Cardiff (Wales).

In addition to this seven, Network Rail also has four control centres: Swindon (Western); London (South East, Kent); Derby (LNE Midlands); and Glasgow (Scotland). So that makes up eleven locations which are recognised as route controls, but there is more: besides this eleven, there is the National Operating Centre (NOC) at Milton Keynes, another NOC in London, a control centre at Ashford for services on High Speed One, a West Midlands control centre, a dedicated control centre for Merseyrail services at Sandhills and big signalling hubs such as Edinburgh Integrated Electronic Control Centre (IECC).

As if that was not complicated enough, there is the prospect of what is known as the Digital Railway to be taken into account in looking at the future of UK railway signalling. This is a proposal for the adoption of digital train control sometime in the next 25 years, using in-cab signalling (called the European Train Control System) in place of visual signalling in order to optimise the speed and movement of trains on the network, so that they can be run at shorter headways – the minimum amount of time between each train on a section of line.

Mechanical signalling: a timetable for replacement

Schedules showing planned replacement dates for Britain's remaining mechanical signalling have been published and revised numerous times, and in many cases, dates slip and signallers I have spoken to hear different dates to what has appeared in print. So I sought help from Network Rail in confirming what replacement is planned in Control Period (CP5) which ends in April 2019, what schemes are planned for CP6 (April 2019-March 2024) and finally, how much mechanical signalling would remain at the end of CP6.

Starting with clarification of what remains, my Network Rail document (dated 22 September 2017) confirms that there is a current total of 337 operational mechanical or electro-mechanical signal boxes on the national network, a relatively modest reduction from the total of 373 it had announced at the start of 2015. Those 337 boxes currently control a total of 1,543 semaphore signals, with by far the largest concentrations being in four regions – the North-East (298), North-West (325), Scotland (261) and Wales (243) – as is reflected in the subsequent chapters of this book.

In the Control Period running up to April 2019 (CP5), there were five principal schemes that are expected to be completed. In England, these are the Wherry Line routes from Norwich to Great Yarmouth and Lowestoft, Preston to Blackpool North and Gilberdyke to Ferriby on Humberside. In Scotland, the focus is on the Aberdeen-Inverness route, where the biggest change is at Forres, with its station re-sited and signal box abolished – completed on schedule in October 2017 – with work progressively extending along the whole length of the route towards Aberdeen, including a re-doubling of section of line from Inverurie to Aberdeen. Finally, the North Wales upgrade, mentioned earlier, leaves Anglesey, Llandudno and Llanrwst as the final outposts of mechanical signalling in this region.

Semaphore signalling at Moreton-in-Marsh survived re-doubling of the Cotswold Line, completed in 2011, with the station even gaining the short new up starter. It is seen on the left in this 13 February 2017 view as GWR 180106 departs with the 12.06 Worcester Foregate Street-London Paddington.

A trio of working semaphores survives on the Isle of Wight, including the Ryde St. John's Road down home signal, seen here on 28 December 2016 as 483008 passes with a Shanklin-bound service

Moving on to CP6 (2019-24), the schedule supplied to me by Network Rail showing its priority schemes (all still subject to funding) is more notable for what is *not* included than for the schemes regarded as its top priorities. Among relatively few schemes listed, this period will see the elimination of semaphore signalling at Tondu and Park Junction in South Wales, while a project called Port Talbot West phase 2 will spell the end of semaphore signalling on the South Wales main line when Pembrey & Burry Port and Ferryside boxes are eliminated.

Upgrading work in Scotland is due to see closure of Cupar Signal Box and electrification of the route from Dunblane to Perth which would entail the loss of some notable boxes, at Auchterarder, Hilton Junction and Barnhill, as well as what would then be one of only two remaining co-acting signals at Geenloaning, following the loss of one at Cantley as part of the Wherry Lines re-signalling.

Another major loss of mechanical signalling will come during CP6 through what is called by Network Rail the Durham Coast Type F project. This will complete the elimination of semaphore signalling on the route from Newcastle via Sunderland to Middlesbrough and lead to closure of Britain's oldest signal boxes – Norton South and Norton East – along with the fine boxes at Norton-on-Tees and Billingham featured in chapter six.

What is not in the CP6 schedule are some major sections of route where re-signalling has long been anticipated, notably the Great Western Main Line in Cornwall, the Marches Line between Shrewsbury and Newport, the Leicester to Peterborough route, as well as major surviving stretches of line featured elsewhere, including the Cumbrian Coast, much of the Highland Main Line and the East Coast Main Line from Aberdeen to Dundee.

Network Rail projects that by the end of CP6 in April 2024, the number of mechanical and electro-mechanical signal boxes will be down from the current 337 to a total of 263, but there will still be a remarkable 1,218 surviving semaphore signals at that date.

Manual signalling today and projected picture at the end of CP6

NetworkRail Route	Number of mechanical/ electro-mechanical signal boxes (Sept.2017)	Projected number of mechanical/ electro-mechanical signal boxes at end of CP6 (April 2024)	Number of semaphore signals (Sept. 2017)	Projected number of semaphore signals at end of CP6 (April 2024)
Anglia	25	16	110	44
Kent	8	8	12	12
LNE	70	51	298	221
LNW (N)	86	70	325	279
LNW (S)	2	2	1	1
East Midlands	23	22	94	90
Scotland	56	40	261	200
Sussex	5	4	9	8
Wales	39	29	243	173
Wessex	4	2	23	23
Western	19	19	167	167
TOTAL	337	263	1543	1218

Source: Network Rail/22 September 2017

Looking at this regional analysis of the number of planned signal box closures and reduction in semaphore signals between now and April 2024 (table) makes very interesting reading, with no reduction in the number of mechanical signals at all on four of the twelve Network Rail Routes: Kent, LNW (S); Wessex; and Wales and only minimal change in the East Midlands and Sussex. Of the four major regions for surviving semaphores, the biggest reduction in signal numbers is projected to be in Wales (29 per cent), followed by the LNE Route (26 per cent), with Scotland losing 23 per cent of its remaining mechanical signals and LNW (N) just 14 per cent.

Getting around

In researching this story and photographing signals, boxes and passing trains, I have attempted wherever possible to travel by train, using a wide variety of ticket offers to make my travels as economical as possible. So I owe a debt of gratitude to those train operators whose special offers have helped limit my travel costs.

These have included promotional flat fare offers from Great Western Railway and Virgin Trains, my £172 Ryde Gold Card (an annual season ticket from Ryde Esplanade to Ryde St. John's Road) that has given me free weekend tickets and discounts on South West Trains (now South Western Railway), Club 50 membership with Scotrail, Club 55 from Arriva Trains Wales, a four-day IE 'trekker' ticket in Ireland and numerous ranger tickets, as mentioned in the text.

For those unfamiliar with National Rail ticketing rules and regulations, it is worth remembering that anytime and off-peak return tickets allow for unlimited breaks of journey on the return trip (and outward too, in the case of anytime tickets). That means it is possible to buy just one ticket and visit numerous locations on a section of line, often more cheaply than by use of a day ranger ticket.

While there have been occasions where a car has been essential to visit boxes in remote locations, it is remarkable how high a proportion of the locations featured can easily be reached by train, or in some instances by bus or on foot. As the regional chapters will detail, there are also some interesting walks for the intrepid signalling enthusiast, amongst which I would single out Ribblehead to Blea Moor, Dove Holes to Buxton, Bugle to Goonbarrow Junction, Broomfleet to Brough and Stockton-on-Tees to Billingham.

Not every location lends itself to easy photography however – being of relatively modest stature (5ft 6¾in), there are places where bridge parapets or fencing create great difficulties, with photography from level crossings also proving awkward in many places. Another bugbear has been lineside vegetation. There are many locations where it is possible to find a good and safe vantage point to photograph trains passing signals, only for it to be ruined by trees and shrubs that have been allowed to spread unchecked down the sides of railway cuttings and consequently made a decent shot impossible. Given how secure the railway environment has now been made, it does seem a shame that one is sometimes penalized for not trespassing by Network Rail's failure to keep nature at bay.

In the course of my travels around Great Britain I have been lucky enough to meet a number of signallers who have been happy to answer my questions about the semaphores under their control and, in some cases, to invite me in to their boxes to savour the unique and historic working environment. For that, I owe special thanks to signallers at Ashwell, Crabley Creek, Glenwhilly, Gristhorpe Crossing, North Seaton, Prudhoe, Scropton Crossing and Welton, who all helped me bring this story to life with their priceless insights and anecdotes.

A view of Britain's finest signalling location on 13 May 2017, with the world's largest mechanical signal box, Shrewsbury Severn Bridge Junction, in the background and Abbey Foregate Signal Box in the foreground.

My special thanks also to the individuals at Network Rail who kindly organised an official visit for me during my preparation of this book, particularly Aidan Anderson, Relief Mobile Operations Manager in Preston. This was a visit on Friday, 22 September 2017 to the boxes at Blackpool North, Carleton Crossing and Poulton-le-Fylde, only weeks before they were to finally close on Saturday, 11 November 2017, in preparation for the long awaited and overdue upgrading and electrification of the route from Preston to Blackpool North.

Britain's finest surviving semaphores

As the following chapters will describe and illustrate, there is a surprisingly large number of locations where manual signalling survives. Many are unfortunately difficult to photograph, either because of an isolated location or problems with lineside vegetation and accessibility. Despite these frustrations, there are some delightful places to savour working semaphores, and in touring everywhere from Forres and Elgin in northern Scotland to St. Erth in Cornwall as well as Holyhead and Ferryside in Wales, there are inevitably places which stand out in the memory. So, for what it is worth, here is my Top Twenty:

1. Shrewsbury area – biggest and simply the best!
2. Worcester area – a fine collection of lower quadrant signals
3. Brundall/Cantley/Reedham – three wonderful locations, soon to disappear
4. Knaresborough – a remarkable signal box in an historic setting
5. Blackpool North – the finest seaside terminus of all, now sadly departed
6. Arbroath – another remarkable signal box and variety of photo-spots
7. St. Erth – a busy and charming country junction
8. Craven Arms – another rural junction with a variety of traffic
9. Settle Junction – panoramic views of some spectacular scenery
10. Llandudno/Deganwy – rare signal gantry and attractive locations
11. Liskeard – special signals and an unusual station layout
12. Gilberdyke – semaphore signalling of a main line junction
13. Skegness – a totally unspoiled seaside terminus
14. Parbold – along with nearby Chapel Lane Crossing a delightful surprise
15. Helsby – a charming junction station with a rare co-acting signal
16. Ulverston – attractive listed station and an unusual lay-out
17. Appleby – a fine station and location, untouched by progress
18. Par/St. Blazey – a busy country junction, with numerous photo-spots
19. Norton-on-Tees – panoramic views from a nearby footbridge
20. Moreton-in-Marsh – charming country station with a new semaphore

There are also a number of what I describe as special signals – unusual survivals that are a 'must visit' for those with an interest in our mechanical signalling heritage and which are described and illustrated elsewhere in this book. Foremost of these must be two unique survivals, the remarkable Midland Railway wooden post and lower quadrant semaphore signal at Ketton, near Stamford in Rutland on the route from Peterborough to Leicester and, in neighbouring Lincolnshire, the 'somersault' signal adjacent to the swing bridge on the branch line leading from Boston Docks.

In addition, there are the three surviving co-acting signals on Network Rail. These are signal posts with two arms at locations where an obstruction such as a bridge means the train driver would have difficulty in seeing a single arm at conventional height, so one arm is positioned at low level and one much higher to make it visible from beyond the obstruction.

This trio is located at Cantley, on the Wherry Lines route from Norwich to Lowestoft, at Helsby in Cheshire and, in Scotland, at Greenloaning between Stirling and Perth. In the preservation world, there is a fine example of a much earlier London & South Western Railway lower quadrant co-acting signal, at Ropley on the Mid-Hants Railway.

There are also a number of other unusual signals at four locations on the former Great Western Railway. These are the centre pivot type signals that survive to this day at Liskeard, Worcester Shrub Hill, Droitwich Spa and Shrewsbury. In the preservation world, this type can be seen at Bewdley on the Severn Valley Railway. Other rarities that I have noted on my travels include another wooden post at Hellifield (not totally original, I was told by a local enthusiast) and probably the last surviving over-line semaphore signal gantry on the national network, at Llandudno in North Wales.

Finally, working distant signals are something of a rarity. In Scotland, the only remaining example is at Glenwhilly, there are now just two survivors in North Wales, but in England there are working examples in places such as the Wherry Lines from Norwich to Great Yarmouth and Lowestoft, the Poacher Line from Grantham to Skegness and the Harrogate to York route. Those distant signals mounted below home signals in the Worcester area are all fixed, with the UK's last working lower quadrant distant signal being on the Marches Line just south of Shrewsbury and controlled by Sutton Bridge Junction Signal Box.

This book is very much an enthusiast's eye view of Britain's last surviving mechanical signalling, which has necessarily been limited by my not venturing off platform ends and only sporadically being invited into boxes by signallers willing to discuss their work with me. Nevertheless, I hope it gives a good reflection of our surviving signalling heritage and, as the replacement process eliminates ever more boxes, that some official consideration is given to not just listing the boxes themselves, but the working signals as well.

What an attraction it would be if a route such as the splendid Wherry Lines in Norfolk – self-contained and with no regular freight or long distance traffic – could have been saved for future generations as a working example of Britain's amazing signalling heritage. Alas, though, in August 2017 it was announced that Network Rail had awarded consultants Atkins a £29 million contract to re-signal the entire Wherry Line route, in order that its new digital signalling could be controlled from spring 2019 by Colchester Power Signal Box (PSB).

CHAPTER 1

EAST ANGLIA

Until re-signalling of the Ely-Norwich route was completed at the end of 2012, it was possible to travel across East Anglia from Peterborough on the East Coast Main Line to the resorts of Great Yarmouth and Lowestoft along routes that remained predominantly controlled by mechanical signalling. But a £21 million re-signalling project saw the end of nine signal boxes, among them the oldest and finest being the 1877-vintage Wymondham South Junction box, which survives today, albeit redundant, at a junction west of Wymondham station with the preserved Mid-Norfolk Railway to Dereham.

So for a tour of East Anglia's remaining manual signalling, we will begin our journey at Peterborough on the East Coast Main Line and head first towards another important railway junction at Ely, before heading north-east along the re-signalled route from there to Norwich and then onto what must undoubtedly be one of the very finest outposts of mechanical signalling anywhere in England, the Wherry Lines to Great Yarmouth and Lowestoft.

Peterborough-Ely

Travelling by rail, rather than with the benefit of a car, there are three locations with mechanical signalling it is possible to visit on this busy section of line. Heading east from Peterborough, the first sign of

Cross Country (XC) 170116 passes Whittlesea's attractive signal box on 30 November 2016 with a westbound XC service to Birmingham New Street.

mechanical signalling is at Kings Dyke, where a small single storey box controls a level crossing on the busy A605 trunk road. Shortly afterwards comes Three Horse Shoes, but neither of these two boxes has any remaining semaphores, so the first semaphores are at a station on the edge of a village called Whittlesey. The station is confusingly called Whittlesea and here an attractive Great Eastern Railway signal box, dating from 1887, stands south of the line to the east of the station, with facing and trailing crossovers close to the box, as well as a disused refuge siding in front of the box.

Whittlesea station has staggered platforms and wooden crossing gates, which are controlled from a modern Portacabin-type building at the west end of the station. There are six semaphore arms visible from the platforms, with a home, starter and section signal in each direction – the eastbound home, however, has a sighting board behind it, so cannot really be seen for a photo. In the westbound direction the section signal (W23) stands only a short distance from starter signal W25, as it protects another nearby level crossing.

Continuing in an easterly direction, March can boast two impressive signal boxes only half a mile apart and a well-preserved station, where two unused platforms on the north side of the station look almost ready to receive the first trains from a re-opened Wisbech, once revival of the seven-mile branch line has finally been approved and funded. Sadly, the only semaphores remaining here are a handful of shunting signals controlling access and exit from little-used sidings to the east of the station between the two signal boxes.

EMT 158865 passes March East Junction Signal Box with a Peterborough-bound service on 30 November 2016. The only remaining semaphores here are shunting signals, including the pair seen in front of the goods shed.

Despite the lack of active mechanical signalling, the boxes at March East Junction – close to the station – and the nearby South box are magnificent survivals and well worth the visit. To walk the half mile from March station to South Junction signal box, take a path from just outside the station heading parallel with the railway. This becomes Willowherb Close and leads into Foxglove Way, which you follow to its junction with Creek Road, before turning left where you will see the signal box and level crossing ahead.

One final location for semaphore signals on this route is Manea (pronounced Maynee) station, a pleasantly quiet spot on the edge of an East Anglian village, with trains only stopping every two hours (although the service is to be increased to hourly in December 2019). The signal box stands at the east end of the station, controlling a level crossing and four semaphore arms: a home (on a bracket) and starter in the eastbound direction and home and starter on the westbound side.

Besides having a good vantage point on the westbound platform, what makes this a great spot is the scale and variety of traffic passing. Passenger services on the line are run by three separate operators – Abellio Greater Anglia, Arriva Cross Country and East Midlands Trains, while there is a steady succession of Class 66-hauled freights, conveying containers to and from Felixstowe as well as a variety of other cargo.

Norwich–Great Yarmouth/Lowestoft (The Wherry Lines)

Anyone looking for a route system that is almost exclusively controlled by semaphore signalling, with a range of attractive signal boxes and locations to visit and photograph, could do no better than visit the Wherry Lines from Norwich to Great Yarmouth and Lowestoft. This 46¼-mile network features nine manual signal boxes, two of which also operate swing bridges, a weekend only request stop,

There is heavy freight traffic on the Ely-Peterborough route. Here 66847 approaches Manea station with a westbound train on 30 November 2016.

and, at Berney Arms, one of the remotest and quietest stations (albeit without any signalling) in the whole of England.

Adding further to the railway interest has been the regular use on these lines of not one but two locomotive-hauled trains, one comprising two Class 68 locos at either end of three coaches and the other being another three coach formation powered by two Class 37 locos. Between them, these two sets have been working services on weekdays, as well as summer Saturdays and make a very pleasant change from the Class 156 two-car units and single coach Class 153s which currently form the bulk of Wherry line services.

Getting to the area by train is very straightforward, with half-hourly express services to Norwich from London and half-hourly services from the Ely direction, one originating at Cambridge and the other a CrossCountry (XC) service from Peterborough and Birmingham. There is a Wherry Lines Day Ranger ticket covering these routes, but for those coming from farther afield and holding a Gold Card (London area annual season ticket) or any other railcard, the cheapest way of getting here without advance booking seems to be a day return to Cambridge then an Anglia Plus Day Ranger Ticket, which covers the Cambridge-Norwich route, the Wherry Lines, as well as the scenic Bittern Line to Cromer and Sheringham, the East Suffolk Line from Lowestoft to Ipswich and all lines in between.

Once at Norwich, the basic pattern of service is hourly services to Great

Loco-hauled trains have been an added attraction on the Wherry Lines in recent years. On 21 December 2016, 37424 departs Brundall with the 12.46 service to Great Yarmouth, with 37405 at the rear.

Yarmouth via Acle and on the main route to Lowestoft, with occasional extra Great Yarmouth services routed via Reedham and Berney Arms, while on Summer Saturdays there are additional hourly non-stop services from Norwich to Great Yarmouth, which are normally routed via Berney Arms and which have featured loco-haulage by Class 37 locomotives top and tailing a "short set" of two or three coaches.

Setting out from Norwich, the double-track line to Lowestoft passes to the north of Crown Point depot and Trowse Junction, where the Bittern Line to Cromer and Sheringham diverges, through Brundall Gardens (a stop omitted by many services) and on to the route's first signal box at Brundall. This charming and

photogenic spot has staggered platforms on either side of a wooden-gated level crossing. As the signal box is located at the far eastern end of the up platform, the level crossing is worked by a controller who is based in a small hut located under a footbridge, which conveniently spans the tracks and makes a great vantage point for photography.

Pausing here on a summer Saturday, you quickly realise what a hectic life the crossing keeper has at Brundall, with up to eight trains passing each hour, each one requiring a separate opening and closing of the substantial wooden crossing gates. From a photographic point of view, the best shots are to be had from the footbridge, with its view of the signal box and junction signals immediately in front

Returning from Great Yarmouth, 37405 is about to pass the Grade II-Listed Brundall Signal Box with one of the two 'short sets' in operation on 21 December 2016 and 37558 at the rear.

of the point where the single-line route via Acle to Great Yarmouth diverges from the main Lowestoft line. Other good shots can be had from the western (Norwich) end of the down platform, with the tall down home signal visible above the footbridge, and at the eastern end of the up platform, close to the signal box.

Taking a trip first along the Acle line, and just 12 minutes from Brundall stands Acle station, which is impressively preserved with old enamel signs adding a period touch to a station which was a past winner of the best kept unstaffed station in the Anglia region. Spending an hour here between trains gives a good chance to appreciate the small signal box, located at the western end of the down platform, another piece of period signage on the

footbridge and semaphores controlling both ends of the station.

Moving on from Acle to the end of the line at Great Yarmouth, or Yarmouth Vauxhall as the signal box is named in recognition of the time when there were other stations in the town, one is reminded of the large volume of holiday traffic once arriving here by long-disused carriage sidings fast disappearing into the undergrowth to the west of the station, yet still guarded by a solitary semaphore. The station itself boasts four long platforms, with a two-arm signal bracket guarding exit from platforms 1 and 2, while single semaphores control departure of trains from platforms 3 and 4. Under each signal is an illuminated route indicator, which will show A for a train routed via the

Abellio 156407 leaves the passing loop at Acle on 3 September 2016 with the 13.28 departure for Norwich.

Abellio 156416 departs Great Yarmouth at 14.17 on 3 September 2016 with a service for Norwich. The A showing in the route indicator below the home signal indicates that it is routed via Acle.

Single unit Abellio 153322 leaves Great Yarmouth on 3 September 2016 with one of the Summer Saturday non-stop services to Norwich. The route indicator R below the signal means that it will run via Reedham.

Acle line and R for those services heading to Norwich via Reedham Junction.

Returning now to Brundall, and a trip from here down the double track main line to Lowestoft first takes you past the little-served station of Buckenham, where a couple of week-end services make request calls for the benefit of those visiting a local bird sanctuary and steam museum. Next up is the charming village of Cantley, dominated by a huge British Sugar beet refinery that once generated important freight traffic to a route where sadly rail-borne freight is no more. This is another very photogenic spot, with the signal box located adjacent to another wooden gated level crossing, this time one that is worked by the signaller and slightly less busy than the one at Brundall.

What makes Cantley rather special is its down outer home signal (C21) which is one of the last three co-acting signals left anywhere in England or Wales – the only other surviving examples on the network being at Greenloaning near Stirling in Scotland and at Helsby in Cheshire. C21 is located just west of the down platform and can easily be viewed and photographed from a pedestrian level crossing just to the west of the village.

Cantley is another of the route's many attractive locations, with a normal pattern of services that sees alternate (i.e. two-hourly) Lowestoft line services call, along with irregular services to and from Great Yarmouth via Berney Arms. For a pleasant way to pass the time between trains, take a visit to the Reedcutter pub, just five

Cantley's down outer home signal (C21) is one of only three surviving co-acting signals on the national railway network. On 8 October 2016 single-car units 153309/335, forming the 12.05 Norwich-Lowestoft service, are about to call at Cantley station.

minutes' walk south from the station alongside the River Yare and a popular stopping-off point for those sailing on the Broads.

Heading 2¼ miles or five train minutes south-east from Cantley brings you to the next and finest mechanical signalling location on the Wherry routes, Reedham Junction. This must-visit location boasts a tall and elegant 1907 Great Eastern Railway signal box standing some distance to the east of Reedham station, surrounded by a collection of around a dozen semaphore signals. These control the station area, and the junction of the two routes to Berney Arms and to Lowestoft, located around a curve some half a mile east of the station, as well as access to Reedham Swing Bridge on the Lowestoft route.

There are a number of easily accessible photographic locations here, starting with the eastern end of either station platform, where there is a fine view of the signal

box and signalling and a tall brick-built road bridge immediately behind the signal box. Taking time to explore the charming village of Reedham is well worthwhile from a signalling viewpoint. A 12-minute walk in an easterly direction from the station brings you to a second road over-bridge (Mill Road) at the point where the two lines divide. While no signalling can be seen looking east – a junction signal for trains from Berney Arms is behind a sighting board – looking back towards the station a number of signals can be seen.

Immediately in front of you and on the left hand side are home and distant signals on a concrete post. This is a section signal from Reedham Junction with a motor worked distant below, controlled by Reedham Swing Bridge signal box. To the right is a motor worked section signal for the Berney Arms route, while some distance away are up home signals for the Berney Arms route (R54) and the Lowestoft line (R58).

Abellio 156407 passes Cantley's down home (C3) on 8 October 2016 with the 12.58 fast service from Norwich to Lowestoft.

DRS-owned 37423
Spirit of the Lakes
(front) and 37425
*Sir Robert McAlpine/
Concrete Bob* (rear)
approach Reedham
on 17 March 2017
with the 15.48
Lowestoft to
Norwich service.

Abellio 156409
approaches
Reedham Junction
on 17 March 2017
with the 15.17
Great Yarmouth to
Norwich service, one
of the few weekday
services routed via
Berney Arms.

Carry on down Mill Road from this bridge and bear left at Reedham Primary School, which brings you to another road over-bridge where there is a great view looking south onto the swing bridge. While looking north, where the double track sweeps round to the left, there is the Reedham Junction distant signal (R60) on the left and a tall home signal protecting the swing bridge on the right.

There is one final vantage point for Reedham's splendid semaphore signals and this can be reached using a path to the east of this railway bridge from where a five minute walk alongside what was once a wartime eastern side of the railway triangle takes you to a level crossing on the Berney Arms route. Here, an up distant (R56) can be seen in one direction – though not easily photographed – while looking towards the Mill Road bridge and Reedham station gives you a view of the outer home signal (R55).

After passing through the unsignalled station at Haddiscoe, the next interesting location on this route is the line's second swing bridge – this time a crossing of the River Waveney – beyond which the line sweeps round to the right and into Somerleyton station, another quiet and attractive spot and another place served only by alternate hourly services on the Lowestoft route. This is a pleasantly photogenic spot, with a tall down starting signal (SB9) standing on the right hand side of the line opposite the end of the down platform, and an up outer home on an unusual concrete post (SB12) at the end of the up platform.

Abellio 170208 passes Brundall's Acle line up distant signal BL35 on 20 July 2018, with the 12.17 Great Yarmouth – Norwich service.

DRS-owned
68001 (front) and
68025 approach
Somerleyton
Swing Bridge on
21 December 2016
with the 10.57
Lowestoft-Norwich.
Note SB12's unusual
concrete post.

Abellio 156417
comes off
Somerleyton
Swing Bridge on
21 December 2016
with the fast 10.58
Norwich-Lowestoft.

Looking towards Lowestoft from the eastern end of the up platform, as the line sweeps round a left hand bend, there is a trailing crossover, with an advanced down starter visible in the distance. From the western end of the platforms at Somerleyton station, there is a good view of the swing bridge signal box and the semaphore arms protecting it in each direction, with the one in the up direction (SB8), like the up starter, also being on a concrete post.

Replacement of signal boxes on the Wherry Lines had been slated for 2015 but is now scheduled for early 2019. This programme does not, apparently, include the two swing bridge boxes – somehow, the thought of these bridges being controlled remotely from Colchester seems quite an alarming prospect! – so either the ageing bridges will ultimately have to be replaced

or, as has been speculated about within the enthusiast community, they might one day be the last manual signal boxes to survive anywhere on the UK rail network.

Nearing the end of our 23½-mile journey from Norwich to Lowestoft, the penultimate calling point on this double track route is Oulton Broad North, a busy town on the outskirts of Lowestoft also boasting another station, Oulton Broad South, on the East Suffolk Line to Ipswich, which diverges from the Norwich-Lowestoft line just east of Oulton Broad North station. It seems slightly ironic that the junction onto a route which was one of the pioneers of RETB (Radio Electronic Token Block) signalling is still controlled by semaphore signals!

Oulton Broad North has an attractive 1901 Great Eastern Railway signal box, standing

A large crowd waits on the up platform at Oulton Broad North on 8 October 2016 as Abellio 156412 passes the East Suffolk Line Junction and approaches the station with the 14.57 Lowestoft-Norwich.

Abellio 170208 passes the Lowestoft distant signal (L59) as it nears Oulton Broad North Junction on 8 October 2016 with the 15.07 East Suffolk Line service from Lowestoft to Ipswich.

across a busy main road from the station and controlling a barrier level crossing. It is yet another interesting photographic location, where the main station building on the eastbound (Lowestoft) platform survives in a new guise as an Indian take-away restaurant. There are good shots to be had from both ends of this platform and an even better view, of the station and East Suffolk Line junction, from a footbridge east of the station. This can be reached by walking down a nearby cul-de-sac called Harbour Road, then continuing along a rough path through some waste ground adjacent to the line.

Finally, to Lowestoft itself – or more correctly Lowestoft Central as the delightful early BR (Eastern Region) blue enamel sign on the station building proclaims. Sadly, the station is a shadow of what it once was, with the station roof completely removed, although the station itself remains staffed and busy. Like nearby Great Yarmouth there are three platform roads, the exit from platform two being controlled by a single arm and a two-arm bracket controlling exit

from platforms three and four, with an attractive signal box some 100 yards up the line. There are a number of sidings to the south of the passenger lines, which remain connected and signalled, although it looks a considerable time since the last rail-borne fish traffic left the port!

Despite confirmation of its planned replacement, I cannot help feeling that the Wherry Line's marvellous signalling represents an excellent opportunity to take the process of listing our signalling heritage to a new level. Having travelled the length and breadth of Britain to view our remaining manual signalling, I am more than ever convinced that listing signal boxes in isolation is not sufficient. What is needed now is for a section of mechanical signalling to be listed as a working tribute to our Victorian railway heritage. The system is safe and reliable and the Wherry Lines – self-contained, with no high speed or freight services and significant tourist potential – would be the ideal place for the listing of not just boxes, but of the entire signalling infrastructure.

Abellio 156417 passes Lowestoft Signal Box on 8 October 2016 with the 14.17 Ipswich-Lowestoft East Suffolk Line service.

Just two weeks before their displacement from East Anglian duties, DRS-owned 68005/028 depart Lowestoft on 23 August 2017 with the 10.57 service to Norwich.

CHAPTER 2

SOUTH OF ENGLAND

While East Anglia and every other part of Great Britain continue to boast outposts of mechanical signalling, the second decade of the twenty-first century has seen it all but eliminated from the South of England's railway network. After three notable re-signalling projects undertaken between 2011 and 2015, there are (at the time of writing) just ten locations across the whole of the south with any surviving semaphore signals, all single boxes, with the exception of a short stretch of lightly-used freight-only line in North London.

One of this ten has a solitary signal, used once a day to control the departure of a 'ghost train' service, while another stands on the freight-only route from Southampton to Fawley, that in 2016 lost most of its traffic with the cessation of oil tank trains to the Fawley refinery. All but two of the ten control solely upper quadrant signals, with one remaining box (Greenford East) having Great Western-style lower quadrant signals and one box (Yeovil Pen Mill) a mixture of the two.

Despite this seemingly bleak picture, for the dedicated enthusiast, a tour of this huge region can still prove rewarding. Among highlights, it gives you an excuse to take a ride on a daily 'Parliamentary' train, the opportunity to watch high speed 'Javelin' trains being signalled by Victorian technology, and a chance to go offshore and see Britain's oldest rolling stock fleet in action on the charming Isle of Wight.

The first of three re-signalling projects to have virtually wiped out the south's semaphores was Phase 1 of a re-signalling project in East Kent, completed at the end of 2011. It covered a sizeable swathe of the county east of Sittingbourne towards Dover and led to the loss of signal boxes controlling semaphores at Canterbury East and Shepherdswell, along with other significant changes, as the area was brought under the control of one of Network Rail's planned new Railway Operating Centres.

Second of the three schemes to have been completed since 2010 was a scenic southern stretch of the Mid-Sussex line, which led to the closure in March 2014 of manual boxes at Billingshurst, Pulborough and Amberley. Both Billingshurst and Pulborough boxes are listed structures, with the former having been moved to the Amberley Chalk Pits Museum shortly after closure. Amberley was a delightful small box located on the station's down platform that for many years had been 'switched out' until increased service frequencies on the route had required its regular opening.

Finally, the most extensive closure of the decade took place in February 2015, when seven signal boxes along the East Coastway route between Brighton and Hastings – those at Berwick, Polegate, Hampden Park, Eastbourne, Pevensey and Westham, Normans Bay and Bexhill – all closed and new signalling was commissioned, as control of the route was taken over by another of the new signalling centres, at Three Bridges, between Crawley and Gatwick Airport on the London-Brighton main line.

Greater London: Greenford East

So beginning a clockwise tour of the south's surviving semaphores, the first notable location is Greenford in North West London, a busy stop on London Underground's Central Line and terminus of a half hourly Great Western Railway

shuttle service from West Ealing. Travel here on a West Ruislip-bound Central Line service and for a lengthy part of the journey – from North Acton to South Ruislip – a little used and partly single track railway line runs alongside, with a number of semaphore signals to be seen as the tube train approaches Greenford station.

This is what was once grandly known as the New North Main Line, but is now less glamorously known as the Acton to Northolt line, running for a total distance of 11 miles from just west of Old Oak Common depot on the Great Western Main Line to a junction with the Chiltern Railways route from London Marylebone at South Ruislip.

What was once a major inter-city route, that was built by the Great Western and Great Central Railways, opening in 1903 to provide faster access to London for expresses from places like Birmingham and Birkenhead, is today a strangely neglected part of the UK's rail network, until December 2018 a diversionary route, for the turning of GWR's HST fleet via the

east side of the Greenford triangle, and by a solitary Chiltern Railways passenger train on weekdays only.

Like other 'Parliamentary' or 'ghost trains', the 10.57 South Ruislip to Paddington and 11.36 return to South Ruislip and West Ruislip (at the time of my visit, but now operating to and from West Ealing) is not actually operated for the benefit of passengers, but merely to sustain the route knowledge of Chiltern Railways crews and to avoid the huge cost of trying to implement a formal closure of the line to passenger services.

For a bit of one-upmanship, those with a penchant for unusual railway journeys would not be disappointed if they turned up on Platform 3 at South Ruislip at around 10.30 on a weekday morning, when a two-coach Chiltern Railways Class 166/6 unit was standing waiting to take you in splendid isolation on a sedate 14-mile, 26-minute trip to London Paddington.

My Monday morning journey on the 10.57 from South Ruislip in early December 2016 was probably typical of this curious service. There were three members of

Chiltern Railways' Parliamentary service – the 10.57 from South Ruislip to London Paddington – passes Greenford East's up home signals on 28 November 2016.

crew – a guard and two people in the driver's cab, but I was the only passenger. The journey was rather sedate but did offer the chance to see the remains of the second track between Northolt and Greenford – the route was largely singled in the early 1990s – and the fine collection of lower quadrant semaphore signals operated by Greenford East Signal Box.

Greenford East box, dating from 1904, is a remarkable survivor, which almost certainly owes its longevity to the limited and sporadic nature of the passing services. It controls a triangular junction off the Acton-Northolt route, with the western curve being used by the half-hourly shuttle from West Ealing, although all signals on that side of the triangle are now colour lights. A two-signal bracket (GE41 and GE45) faces the platform at Greenford station, although a line of vegetation between the Underground and Network Rail lines makes photographing the 'Parliamentary' service a challenge.

The signal box itself can be seen and photographed from an access road to it off Rockware Avenue, close to the railway station, and the down home signal (GE55) can also be seen from nearby. But the best and almost only view of Greenford's semaphores, albeit a rather distant one, is to be had from the western end of Perivale underground station, where the two-signal bracket controlling the east junction (GE68 & GE56) can be seen alongside the up advanced starter (GE42). Finally, when travelling towards Greenford from West Ealing, it is possible to see a home signal (GE67) on the east side of the triangle, close to Greenford South Junction.

Greater London: the Dudding Hill Line

Within a few miles of Greenford East is the one line in the whole of the south that remains signalled by semaphores, although one where services are sparse and photographing is tantalisingly difficult. This is what is known as the Dudding Hill Line, a four-mile long freight-only link which diverges

GBRf 66768 passes Dudding Hill Junction, near Cricklewood, on 4 September 2017 with a trainload of oil tanks running from Theale to Immingham.

from the North London Line at Acton Wells Junction, close to North Acton underground station before heading in a clockwise arc passing junctions with the West Coast Main Line at Harlesden, the Chiltern Railways route at Neasden to end in a triangular junction with the Midland Main Line at Cricklewood.

There are three signal boxes along the route, at Acton Canal Wharf, Neasden Junction and at Dudding Hill Junction, which stands at the western end of the triangular junction at Cricklewood. This is the only one of the trio that can easily be photographed from a public vantage point, although there are no semaphore arms within the vicinity, the nearest (and only one) being some distance to the south and visible from Gladstone Park, through which the line passes. This is signal DH12, a down starting signal, with the Neasden Junction distant signal beneath it.

Starting an attempt to photograph signals along the route at its southern end, and travelling on foot and by bus, there seems no way at all of getting to Acton Canal Wharf signal box but, from the Grand Union Canal towpath, it is possible to see a tall and modern home signal protecting the northbound direction. Moving on (by 226 bus) towards Neasden it is possible to see the top of Neasden

Junction signal box from a road called Wharton Close, as well as photograph some of its signals through the trees, including a fine pair of signals (NJ23 & NJ19) protecting the route's junction with the Chiltern Railways line.

A single starting signal in the southbound (down) direction can also be seen at this point, and my visit in the early afternoon of 28 November 2016 was rewarded when the signal was pulled off and GBRf-liveried 66760 *David Gordon Harris* trundled past (there is a ruling 30mph speed limit along the line) with a southbound aggregates train. Quite what the future holds for this now 150-year-old line (it opened in October 1868) is far from clear and, while it has occasionally featured in proposals for new orbital passenger services, nothing has yet materialised, so its twilight existence looks set to continue for the foreseeable future.

Deal

When the East Kent re-signalling of 2011 was completed, it curiously left an isolated outpost of mechanical signalling at Deal, where an attractive 1847 station building is complemented by an equally interesting and appealing 1939 art deco style signal

One of the few signals on the Dudding Hill line that can be seen is the Neasden Junction down (westbound) starter – seen here on 28 November 2016 as GBRf 66760 *David Gordon Harris* passes with an aggregates train.

Britain's fastest domestic trains, the Class 395 Javelin sets, are briefly controlled by semaphore signals as they pass Deal. Here, 395021 departs with the 12.31 to St. Pancras International via Dover on 12 November 2016.

A rail-head treatment train (RHTT) is in action as it approaches Deal Signal Box on 12 November 2016, in the hands of GBRf 66730 (front) and 66726 (rear).

box, known as a Southern Railway Type 13, standing at a level crossing just a short walk north of the station. This is one of many such boxes built by the Southern Railway in what is known as the Odeon or glasshouse style. Deal signal box has been modelled by Hornby and another similar working example can be found at Bognor Regis (see below).

From an enthusiast point of view, what makes Deal fascinating is the chance to see the fastest trains on our domestic rail network – the Class 395 'Javelin' units operating services to and from St. Pancras International via the High Speed One route – being controlled by semaphore signals! Deal station has a down (northbound) home (EBZ40) and an up starter (EBZ6) with an up section signal (EBZ27) visible (but sadly not able to be photographed, except from a passing train) which can be glimpsed, along with a down outer home signal, from a path alongside the line in Victoria Park.

Hastings

Continuing our clockwise tour of England's south coast in search of mechanical signalling, the next port of call is Hastings, a station which shares with Harrogate in North Yorkshire the distinction of having semaphore control at one end of the station and colour lights at the other. While the attractive 1931 neo-Georgian station building was sadly demolished and replaced by a rather less pleasing structure in 2004, the Southern Railway box from 1930 happily survives at the eastern end of the station.

Hastings is a busy four-platform station served by South Eastern services from London via Tonbridge and Southern Railway services from Brighton and from London via Eastbourne. In an easterly direction, many services not being turned at nearby sidings continue on to terminate at Ore, while there are also hourly 'Marshlink' services to Rye and Ashford International.

Nearing the end of its journey, 377404 passes Hastings Signal Box and its eastbound starting signals on 12 November 2016 with the 14.14 to Ore. Note the up home signals behind sighting boards beyond the road bridge.

Two semaphore brackets in front of the signal box control services in the Ore direction, with EDL5 & EDL10 serving platforms 4 and 3 respectively, while EDL6 and EDL7 control exit from platforms 2 and 1. To the east of the station stands a three-arm bracket controls entry to the station, but sighting boards make it impossible to photograph from the station and there appears to be no publicly accessible vantage point to see these signals face on.

Newhaven Marine

Like the Chiltern Railways 'Parliamentary' train to Paddington featured above, Newhaven Marine is another quirk of the British railway system, and particularly the protracted and costly procedure for closing any line or station. The station itself, which served as a convenient

interchange with cross-channel ferry services to Dieppe, has not been open to passengers since August 2006, due to safety concerns about the condition of its now demolished platform canopy.

Technically, the station is not closed however, although any rail-borne ferry passengers are now directed to a connecting bus from Newhaven Town station or can make the 150 yard walk from Newhaven Harbour station. Yet at shortly before 8.00pm every weekday evening, the 19.23 Southern Rail service from Brighton to Newhaven Harbour makes the short journey onwards to Marine station (without passengers), before returning empty stock at 20.15 and, in so doing, passing the station's semaphore home signal (NH35), controlled by nearby Newhaven Harbour signal box, its only remaining semaphore signal.

Newhaven Marine station – behind Newhaven Harbour Signal Box – has just been demolished as 313216 passes the one remaining semaphore signal here (NH35) at 20.15 on 24 May 2017 with the 'ghost train' 5F30 - running empty stock to Brighton.

Quite how much longer this curious situation will continue is something of a mystery. In response to a request under the Freedom of Information Act in February 2016, Joe Kerrigan, Programme Advisor – Stations at the Department for Transport, pointed out that in normal circumstances Network Rail would be obliged to carry out repairs to make the station safe for use. In this case, however, the station buildings (since demolished) were the property of a third party, with NR merely leasing the platform. Kerrigan added that Newhaven Marine is not 'closed' and that should NR wish to propose its closure, it would have to follow the statutory closure procedure set out in the Railways Act 2005.

Littlehampton

When the last three manual signal boxes on the Mid-Sussex line disappeared in March 2014, it was curiously not the complete end of semaphore signalling on this route. At both seaside termini served by trains on this line – Littlehampton and Bognor Regis – semaphore signalling survives, along with two very different, but equally interesting, signal boxes.

The older of this duo is Littlehampton, now a Grade II listed structure and dating from 1886, when it was built to a London, Brighton & South Coast Railway (LB&SCR) Type 2 design, and containing a 1901 LB&SCR lever frame. This is one of the principal reasons for its listed status, along with its overall intactness and its being the only box of its type to survive with its original eaves valancing – the wooden decorative feature seen just below the roof-line in my photo of the box.

Littlehampton has four semaphore arms, two on each of two brackets

313206 departs Littlehampton on 20 August 2016 with a local service to Bognor Regis.

A full gas holder adds to the period scene as 377408 passes Littlehampton's listed signal box on 20 August 2016.

controlling exit from the compact four-platform station, with the signal box standing on the east side of the line immediately north of the station, but only partially visible due to the right hand bend in the track on leaving the station. There is a carriage washer and carriage sidings on the west side of the line and a nearby gas holder adds an historic aspect to the location. For a front view of the signal box, and its faded Network SouthEast vintage name-board, turn right on leaving the station and walk along Terminus Road until opposite the box.

Bognor Regis

As signal boxes go, there could scarcely be a bigger contrast than between the small 1886 structure at Littlehampton and the 1938-vintage art deco 'Odeon' style box at nearby Bognor Regis, which

is another example of the Southern Railway Type 13 design, like the one at Deal, and reckoned to be amongst the most significant signal box designs of the twentieth century. Like the one at Littlehampton, it is adorned with a faded name board dating from the Network SouthEast era of the late 1980s.

Bognor Regis station feels a lot more spacious than Littlehampton, with carriage sidings alongside the station rather than to the north, but has a number of similarities, with two semaphore brackets once again controlling exit from the four platform faces. Neither Bognor nor Littlehampton has any mechanical signalling controlling access to the stations. The signal box stands at the station throat, some distance north of the platforms, but for a closer view, there is a footbridge over the line which can be reached by walking along Longford Road, to the west of the station until just past the box itself.

Another view of 377408, this time departing from Bognor Regis on 20 August 2016 and approaching the 1938-built 'Odeon' style signal box, an identical design (SR13) to the one at Deal.

The complex track layout at Bognor Regis, as seen on 20 August 2016 from a bridge close to the signal box, and showing its four surviving semaphore home signals.

Marchwood

After featuring in a notable 2009 report by the former Association of Train Operating Companies (ATOC) as one of the hottest prospects for re-opening to passenger traffic, the future of the Southampton-Hythe railway line, which had an intermediate station at Marchwood, has been called into question by the ending of oil trains to the Fawley refinery in summer 2016, one of the principal sources of traffic on a route which lost its passenger services in February 1966.

Marchwood station looks remarkably intact for a place which has not seen passenger use for more than 50 years. That is because it has remained the only passing place on the freight-only route to Fawley since then and is also junction for a line serving the 225-acre Marchwood Military Port, which still sees regular freight traffic and has been the subject of speculation about future development following the takeover of its management by a company called Solent Gateway, which is committed to looking at ways of exploiting its commercial potential.

Signalling around Marchwood station is controlled from a frame in the old station building. It comprises five pairs of semaphore signals, one to protect the north of the level crossing at the former station, one protecting the crossing from the south, with two more visible from the crossing. Of particular note from the crossing are the old London & South

Freightliner 66534 OOCL *Express* pulls out of Marchwood and is about to pass up starter MW21 on 10 December 2018, with a trainload of empty container carrying wagons from the nearby port bound for Southampton Container Terminal.

Western Railway finials above these two pairs of signals, in contrast to the modern tubular gantry to the south of the old station.

Ryde (Isle of Wight)

Given that its rolling stock fleet dates from 1938 and is therefore the oldest on the entire UK rail network, it is rather appropriate that some semaphore signalling survives on the 8.4-mile long Island Line, from Ryde Pier Head to Shanklin. This small part of the once extensive (55-mile) island network was saved and electrified in 1967, but even what remains has since suffered substantial rationalisation, as passenger numbers have dwindled and operating losses have spiralled.

Today the island's one remaining signal box is at the south end of Ryde St. John's Road station, headquarters of the line and site of a depot where the fleet of two-car Class 483 units is maintained. There are three working semaphore signals left in the vicinity of St. John's Road station – a down home and starter and an up home signal. The up starter is a two-aspect colour light (WFP14) but there are two further semaphore arms, in the form of fixed distant signals, at either approach to the station.

Photographing these remaining signals is relatively easy. Taking the five from north to south, there is a good shot of the double track leading to Ryde Tunnel and

Pre-war (1938) tube trains provide services on the remaining 8½ mile route from Ryde Pier Head to Shanklin on the Isle of Wight. Here 483004 passes one of the line's two fixed distant signals on 28 December 2016 as it approaches Ryde St. John's Road.

Set 483008 has just passed the Ryde St. John's Road up home signal and is about to call at the station on 28 December 2016 with a train for Ryde Pier Head.

the down fixed distant to be had from the overbridge on Rink Road, while the down home can be photographed from the Park road overbridge, close to the Isle of Wight bus museum, which is housed in a former Southern Vectis bus depot.

Ryde St. John's Road station is a rather charming photo location, with three platform faces and rolling stock dumped or stored outside the adjacent depot. The down starter has a couple of shunting signals for accessing the depot and stands opposite the signal box. Photographing the up home signal is tricky, but there is a reasonable vantage point if you walk down Quarry Road to the west of the railway and continue some way along a path beside the line. This also eventually leads to a foot crossing of the line, from where there is a good view of the up (fixed) distant.

Yeovil Pen Mill

Despite being originally scheduled for replacement during 2016, Yeovil Pen

Mill signal box remains an isolated outpost of semaphore signalling in the south of England, where the nearest surviving manual signals are those at Liskeard in Cornwall and at Marchwood on the freight-only Fawley branch near Southampton (featured above). Pen Mill is a delightful station, standing on the eastern side of the town alongside the Pittards leather goods factory, with relatively easy opportunities to photograph signalling at either end of the station and an excellent pub close by (the Pen Mill Hotel) to pass the time between trains.

Semaphore signalling at Pen Mill was partially replaced in 2009, leaving a curious situation today where there is a trio of recently-installed upper quadrant signal brackets for trains heading south towards Weymouth or Yeovil Junction and a trio of traditional GWR/Western Region single arm lower quadrant signals comprising two home signals south of the station – one on the route from Weymouth (YPM1) and one on the connection from Yeovil Junction – and

GWR 150243 is about to arrive at Yeovil Pen Mill with the late-running 13.20 departure for Weymouth on 16 December 2016. Note new upper quadrant signals in the down (southbound direction) with a traditional lower quadrant signal (YPM4) on the up side of the line.

A view of the unusual layout at Yeovil Pen Mill on 18 June 2016 as HST 43129 (43161 rear) departs with the seasonal 'Weymouth Wizard' Summer Saturday service from Bristol Temple Meads to Weymouth.

an up starter (YPM4) standing 100 yards beyond the signal box at the north end of the station.

Pen Mill station has a curious layout with three platform faces, although when trains use the up line, flanked by platforms 1 and 2, only the train doors on platform 1 are normally opened. Platform 3 is the eastern side of the island platform and is normally used by Weymouth-bound services and by the irregular South Western Railway services from Waterloo to Yeovil Junction that have travelled via Westbury and Castle Cary.

To the south end of the station, the two twin arm signal brackets are the one protecting platform 3 with YPM63 (Weymouth) and YPM59 (Yeovil Junction) while controlling platforms 1 and 2 are YPM61 (Weymouth) and YPM60 (Yeovil Junction). The third replacement bracket is some distance to the north of the station, best seen and photographed (with permission) from the Lazenby builder's yard near the signal box, where YPM64 gives access to platform 3 and YPM62 to platforms 1 and 2.

CHAPTER 3

SOUTH-WEST ENGLAND

Growing up as a schoolboy train spotter in Cheltenham Spa during the 1960s and early 1970s, I had witnessed the disappearance of semaphore signalling in places like Cheltenham and Gloucester during implementation of what was known as the Gloucester and later the Bristol Multiple Aspect Signalling (MAS) schemes between 1968 and 1971, while further south-west, the replacement of semaphores with colour lights had reached Plymouth by the mid-1980s. So it came as a very pleasant surprise to discover that across the Tamar, semaphore signalling had survived on 56 miles of the main line from Liskeard to St. Erth, as well as on the 20¾ mile branch from Par to Newquay.

Cornwall had long remained a blank in my rail travels around Britain, but I had put that to rights on a summer Saturday in 2013, fulfilling a long-cherished plan by covering the entire 268-mile Cornish rail network in a single day, using a £10 Ride Cornwall ticket. My account of that 15-hour, 15-train marathon was later published in *Railway Magazine*, shortly after the Royal Duchy was reconnected to the rest of the British railway network following the devastating breach to the sea wall at Dawlish that had isolated Cornwall in February and March 2014.

During that day trip, I had woken up to the photographic potential of Cornish semaphore signalling by the sight of the unusual up starting signal at Liskeard, the semaphore controlled junctions at Lostwithiel, Par and St. Erth and by the two impressive boxes on the Newquay branch – St Blazey and Goonbarrow Junction – the latter being the place where the High Speed Train I was travelling on (the *Atlantic Coast Express*) had passed a XC Voyager unit working a train from Newquay to the north of England, so a place I was eager to re-visit on a summer Saturday.

I had taken the chance to photograph some of the remaining mechanical signalling on that glorious summer day, notably at St. Erth, Truro and Par, but my second opportunity to capture the period scene came in rather different circumstances on a weekend visit in November 2016, when I once again took advantage of the wonderful Ride Cornwall ticket (now £13.00) to re-visit locations I had passed through three years earlier. A third visit, in June 2017, took me by bus to Goonbarrow Junction, in order to finally photograph the summer Saturday scene when trains cross there, and on foot from Par to St. Blazey, another fascinating and historic location.

How much longer this charming outpost of lower quadrant signalling will survive is the subject of some speculation. One pointer has been the long-awaited replacement of HSTs on the Great Western Railway by the bi-mode IEP Class 802 sets, with all 36 sets due to be in traffic by March 2019. Another sign that the end might be nigh for the Royal Duchy's mechanical signals was an announcement in June 2017 that WS Atkins had secured a £9 million signalling contract for upgrading the section of line from Truro to St. Erth as part of what is called the Cornwall Capacity Enabling Scheme (CCES), which will enable the operation of half-hourly services between Plymouth and Penzance.

Liskeard

Heading south-west from Plymouth, the Duchy's semaphore interest begins at

GWR single car Class 153 units 153329/333 leave Liskeard on 19 November 2016 with the 09.49 departure for Penzance.

Liskeard, 17¾ miles west of Plymouth and junction for the highly scenic Looe Valley branch line, which runs from a platform (No. 3) standing at 90 degrees to the main line and decked-out in 1960s chocolate and cream signage, but sadly without any signalling interest. Close to the Looe platform is the most interesting feature of Liskeard station, an extremely rare wooden arm that is the up starting signal (LD3). This so-called 'gallows' signal is one of only a handful of surviving Great Western centre-pivot signals, with other examples – pictured elsewhere in this book – at Droitwich Spa, Shrewsbury and Worcester Shrub Hill.

Approaching Liskeard by train from the Plymouth direction, the first of the box's six semaphore arms you will see is an outer home (LD35) which is round a curve leading to Liskeard Viaduct, so not visible from the station. Once off the viaduct, you will pass down home signal LD34 before the box itself and then enter the station. Liskeard Signal Box is an attractive white-painted Great Western Railway wooden structure dating from 1915 with a 36-lever frame, at the eastern end of the down platform, opposite LD3 and the junction for Looe.

Standing on the down platform and looking west you will see down starter

LD33 and then advanced starter LD32 on the right hand side of the line for visibility reasons, as the route curves right then left on the approach to Moorswater Viaduct. Beyond view in a westwards direction, up home signal LD2 stands close to Moorswater Viaduct, with a sighting board behind it. Besides these semaphore arms, there are also ground signals controlling trailing crossovers at each end of the station, to allow services from Plymouth to terminate.

Lostwithiel

Continuing our journey westwards, the next station after Liskeard is Bodmin Parkway, formerly Bodmin Road, which lost its signal box in 1985, but remains a junction for the preserved Bodmin & Wenford Railway, with that connection now controlled from the signal box at Lostwithiel, 12½ miles on from Liskeard and the next outpost of mechanical signalling in Cornwall. Lostwithiel's 1893 Great Western Railway (GWR) signal box, with a 63-lever frame, gained a Grade II Listing in 2013 for being one of 26 'highly distinctive' boxes that were selected for

listing in a joint project undertaken by English Heritage and Network Rail.

As at Liskeard, Lostwithiel Signal Box stands at the eastern end of the down platform, from where it controls an adjacent level crossing as well as goods loops beyond, while in the down direction it controls access to the Fowey Branch, which remains open for china clay traffic to the unloading point at Carne Point, near Fowey. There are a good number of semaphore arms visible from the platform of what makes a pleasantly photogenic location.

Approaching on a westbound train, the first signal you will pass is down home LL58, with LL40 controlling exit from the down goods loop. In the up direction, there is a trio of semaphores to look out for, with section signal LL8 quickly followed by LL6 being an advanced starter with a second arm giving access to the up goods loop. Looking east once you are on the platform, you will see up starter LL5 at the platform end opposite the signal box.

Looking west from the down platform and just beyond an impressively tall palm tree stands down starter LL57, with a junction arm for the Fowey branch. Another interesting feature to spot here is

The *Cornish Riviera* departs Liskeard at 10.16 on 19 November 2016, comprising GWR HST power cars 43193 (front) and 43122 (rear) as 150249 arrives with the 10.22 service from Plymouth to Penzance.

XC 221141 approaches Lostwithiel on 19 November 2016 with the 10.48 departure for Manchester Piccadilly.

Passengers await the arrival of GWR 150130 at Lostwithiel on 19 November 2016, which forms the 11.20 departure from Exeter St. Davids for all stations to Penzance.

an early enamel '9 Car' sign in chocolate and cream, dating from the earliest days of diesel multiple unit operation in Cornwall. Beyond the platform ends, up home signal LL3 stands at a point where the line curves to the left and makes for an attractive photo-spot. Beyond this point, and out of view, except from a passing train, are an up outer home signal (LL2) and a signal controlling exit from the Fowey branch (LL4).

Par

Proving that listed signal boxes are like London buses, the other Cornish box to have secured a Grade II accolade in that 2013 Review is just 4½ miles down the line from Lostwithiel, at Par, an important junction for the Atlantic Coast branch line to Newquay and another pleasantly picturesque location. The 1879-vintage GWR box here stands at the southern end of the island platform, where platform 2 is the main up platform and platform 3 is served by trains to and from Newquay, although it is also signalled for use by main line trains from further west.

Par signal box was originally a rather modest affair, built by the GWR in about 1879, but was expanded to its present size in 1893, being doubled in length and subsequently being equipped with a new 57-lever frame in 1913. Later still, it became a beneficiary of signal box closures further west, when an electronic signalling panel was added to give the box control of the main line through nearby St. Austell (whose signal box closed in March 1980 but is still standing) and on past former stations at Burngullow and Grampound Road to Probus and Ladock, another closed station, which is just east of Truro.

XC HST, comprising power cars 43207 (front) and 43304 (rear), pauses at Par with the 19.44 departure for Penzance on 24 June 2017 as GWR 153305/361 stand in platform 3 with the 19.48 departure for Newquay.

GWR 57605 *Totnes Castle* approaches Par on 24 June 2017 with the 17.50 Summer Saturday service from Exeter St. Davids to Penzance, formed of the three seated coaches from the *Night Riviera* sleeper service.

Like Liskeard and Lostwithiel, Par is another photogenic spot, with a convenient pub and recommended overnight stopping point being the Royal Inn, adjacent to the road over-bridge immediately north of the station. By my count, the box here controls some 16 semaphore arms, of which more than half can be seen and photographed from the station, footbridge and road bridge. Looking north from the station, the only signals clearly in view are the main up starter PR54 and the up Newquay starter PR52. Beyond the road bridge, down home PR5 can also be seen, but its junction arm (PR7) for access to platform 3 is obscured by a large poplar tree, with vegetation also obscuring the signal controlling exit from a little used down goods loop (PR30).

But in a south-westerly direction there is a fine view of the main line as it ascends in an S shape passing over Par Viaduct, with down starter PR4 just beyond the platform end and a pair of home junction signals controlling access to platforms 2 (PR55) and 3 (PR50).

Controlling access to the Newquay branch – which is double track as far as nearby St. Blazey – PR8 is the junction signal which stands with platform 3's down home (PR5) immediately in front of the signal box. Just around the tight right hand curve towards St. Blazey stands starter PR9, with St. Blazey's fixed distant below it. Venturing away from the station, a circular walk made by crossing the road bridge and following a path to the right until you reach a path heading right to a bridge under the line gives you a chance to see the down home signal (PR2) with a junction arm alongside for the goods loop.

GWR 150202 stands in Chapel Siding at Par on 25 June 2017, between trips on the Newquay branch, as 43158/153 approach with the 14.03 departure for London Paddington.

GWR 150202 approaches St. Blazey Signal Box on 25 June 2017 with the 11.49 service from Par to Newquay.

St. Blazey

Taking a short detour on our journey westwards through Cornwall, it is well worth making the time to see the two remaining signal boxes along the 20¾ mile branch line from Par to Newquay. The first of these, St. Blazey, is barely half a mile from Par at the end of the sharp right hand bend leading away from Par station, where the box stands on the site of a former station (closed in September 1925) and at the junction of a line leading south and under Par Viaduct on the main line to Par Harbour and to the famous and Grade II Listed turntable and roundhouse.

Getting here on foot takes less than ten minutes, crossing the road bridge north of Par station, then either taking one of the 'clay trails' through some woods to the left or following St. Andrew's Road round to the left and on to Middleway Level Crossing in the village of St. Blazey, north-west of the signal box. St Blazey boasts extensive sidings and is home to a number of DB-branded china clay hoppers. St Blazey Signal Box controls the short double track section of line from Par and has a good number of semaphores – I counted four in the down direction and five in the up direction, as well as shunting discs and a signal for exiting the Par Harbour branch.

There is a range of interesting photo opportunities here, beginning at the level crossing on St. Andrew's Road, the road route from Par station. Here, there is a pair of signals in the up direction (SB2) just beyond the crossing in the Newquay

XC 220006 leaves the passing loop at St. Blazey on 25 June 2017 with the 09.01 service from Plymouth to Newquay.

direction, which offer an attractive view on a straight section of line towards Newquay, with section signal SB36 visible in the distance. Look back from the crossing towards the signal box and you can see both down starter (SB39) and advanced starter SB38. But for a view of the box and signals around it, take a short walk on the path leading from the level crossing between the river and railway. This brings you to a foot crossing of the double track next to down home signal SB40 and from here you can see the box itself and trains pausing alongside to pick up or hand over a single line token for the section to Goonbarrow Junction.

Goonbarrow Junction

Reaching the second signalling location on the Newquay branch at Goonbarrow Junction is straightforward for the rail-borne traveller on most days of the week, as it stands three-quarters of a mile east of Bugle station, one of four request stops on the Newquay branch. That is of little use, however, if you want to see the

most interesting action here, the Summer Saturday crossing of GWR HSTs and XC Voyagers. That is because there are no day-time stopping services on Summer Saturdays, so the rail borne visitor must take the hourly First Kernow 27 bus to Bugle village centre from outside St. Austell station.

Once at Bugle, the signal box and its five semaphores can be seen in the distance from the ungated Molinnis Road level crossing, just east of the station. This is one of a handful of ungated crossings, controlled only by lights, on the Newquay branch, where every train has to come to a complete stop, before proceeding to cross and helps account for the reasons why even High Speed Trains are scheduled to take around one hour to travel non-stop along the 20¾ mile branch!

After some extensive exploration (on a wet Saturday morning!) there appears to be no way of getting closer to the box from the north side of the line, but for those with the time and stamina there is a good vantage point to the east of the signal box, where a foot crossing of the line is very close to down home signal

GWR 150202 approaches Middleway Level Crossing at St. Blazey on 25 June 2017 with the 09.52 Newquay-Par.

GWR HST, comprising power cars 43189/177, stands at Goonbarrow Junction in dismal weather on Saturday, 24 June 2017 with the 09.44 service from Par to Newquay, while XC 220027 passes with the 09.35 Newquay-Dundee.

G25 and the end of the passing loop. To get here is a one and a half mile walk from the traffic lights in the centre of the village close to the Bugle Inn (recommended). Head south-east on Rosevear Road until you pass the entrance to the Imerys Rocks plant, then continue on a good path – another of the Clay Trails – in an anti-clockwise direction until it becomes a narrow grassy path which brings you to the foot crossing.

There seems little evidence of much freight activity here, although there is another line of china clay wagons, parked on the stub of a former branch line and a diesel shunter stands in another of the sidings. The five semaphores here comprise an up home and starter (G1 and G2), down home and starter (G25 and G24) and an up starter on the down side of the loop (G12). Goonbarrow Junction box is a fairly standard looking Great Western Railway structure dating from around 1909, with a 25-lever frame and, since closure of the box at Newquay in 1987, has controlled the section west to the seaside resort on a 'one engine in steam' basis.

Truro

Returning to the main line at Par to resume our westward journey, there is a reminder of how much signalling has already been rationalised in the shape of the long-closed box standing forlornly on the up platform at St. Austell, before our journey takes us over the Kenwyn and Carvedras viaducts that herald our arrival into Cornwall's most important railhead in the attractive city of Truro. Here, the surviving Great Western signal box, dating from 1899, stands next to a level crossing at the eastern end of the station and was known as Truro East until closure of Truro West Signal Box in November 1971.

Looking east from the station, up home signal T6 stands at the platform end, immediately in front of the signal box on the far side of the road, while in the Penzance direction, the down home signal stands at the end of the Carvedras Viaduct, but is not easily photographed, due to a curved sighting board below the signal arm. At the western end of the station, there are no less than four signal arms to

A colourful scene at the western end of Truro station on 20 November 2016 as GWR HST 43017 (front) and 43155 pass the down starting signals with the 10.28 departure for London Paddington.

GWR HST 43130/185 has just passed the down home signal and approaches Truro Signal Box on 19 November 2016 with the *Cornish Riviera* service from London Paddington to Penzance.

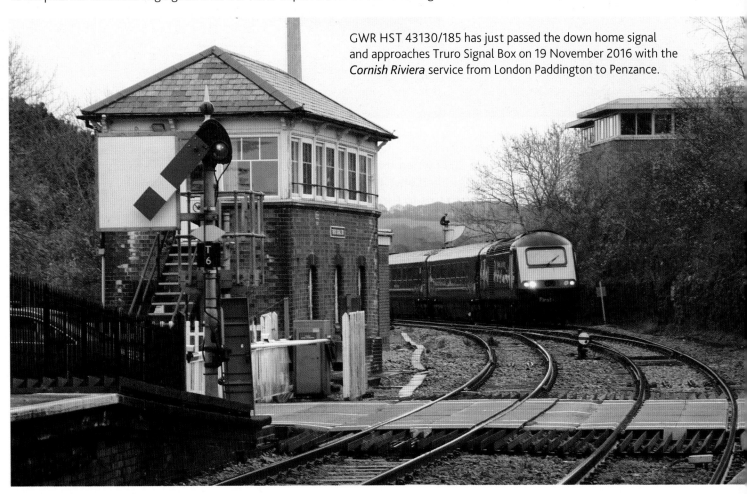

A GWR HST, headed by 43163 *Exeter Panel Signal Box 21st Anniversary 2009*, is about to pass the Truro advanced starter on Sunday, 20 November 2016 with the first up train of the day, the 08.30 Penzance-London Paddington.

be seen, newest of which is T26, which was installed in 2009 when the Falmouth branch was re-signalled and allows Falmouth branch trains to turn back from the up platform. Beyond this quartet, the line curves to the left and there is an up outer home signal (T4) in the cutting leading towards Highertown Tunnel, which does not seem accessible for photos.

Away from the station itself, I found one location well worth exploring for the chance to photograph two semaphore signals standing between the two viaducts (down outer home T50 and up advanced starter T7). It can be reached in ten minutes on foot by heading away from the station, under the Carvedras Viaduct on St. George's Road, bearing right and up a hill on Hendra Road, then sharp right onto Carew Road and continuing until you are close to the line

in Hendra Lane. By climbing onto a low wall, there is the opportunity to photograph trains passing both signals. Worth noting on this walk are the surviving (and listed) stone piers of Brunel's original timber viaduct, alongside the present stone structure.

St Erth

So finally, 56 miles on from Liskeard and 299½ miles from Paddington, our quest for mechanical signalling brings us to Britain's most south-westerly rail junction. St. Erth must also rank as one of its most attractive and unspoiled, with semaphore signalling being the perfect complement to this charming GWR junction station, where even the original footbridge was saved from replacement by a new

structure after a fervent local campaign. It is a busy spot, particularly during the summer, with half-hourly four-car trains on the delightful 4¼ mile branch to St. Ives and main line GWR and XC services calling here at least hourly.

The 1899 GWR signal box stands beyond the railway junction, with the main line passing in front of it and the St. Ives branch behind. Four semaphore arms in view here are down home signal SE2 standing opposite the box, with up home signals on platform 2 being SE66 for the main line and SE64 a junction signal for access to the branch, while beyond this pair the exit from the St. Ives bay platform (3) is controlled by SE9. At the south end of the station there are a trio of signals in view, with down starter SE6 at the end of platform 1, SE54 at the south end of platform 2, for use by branch services continuing to Penzance and using a crossover immediately beyond the signal, and up intermediate home SE67 some 50 yards beyond.

That is not the end of mechanical signalling interest here, as there are two further signals to discover on the branch line. While the St Ives branch home signal is a colour light (SE10), further on towards Lelant Saltings the St. Ives-bound starter (SE62) and St Erth outer home (SE9) – situated at the end of the Lelant Saltings platform – are both semaphores. It seems well worth the 15 minute walk, or £1.00 train fare, to travel on to the popular park and ride stop for a panoramic view of trains travelling along the coast from St. Ives and of St. Erth-bound services passing SE9.

GWR 150216 passes three of the country's most south-westerly semaphore signals as it approaches St. Erth on Sunday, 20 November 2016 with the 11.45 Penzance-St. Ives.

XC 221128 passes St. Erth Signal Box on Sunday, 20 November 2016, with the 12.30 Penzance-Manchester Piccadilly.

On the busy St. Ives branch, the St Erth outer home signal (SE9) stands at the end of the platform at Lelant Saltings, seen here on 23 June 2017 as GWR 150106/121 depart for St. Erth.

WALES & BORDERS

Manual signalling in Wales and the Borders can be summed up as being in three parts. Firstly, there were (at the time of writing) significant stretches of semaphore signalling along some 75 miles of the North Wales coast main line between Holyhead and Chester, secondly there is the fine sequence of boxes and signals on the Marches line south from Shrewsbury to Abergavenny, and finally there are a quintet of isolated spots in the south, at Park Junction (Newport), Pantyfynnon, Tondu, Pembrey & Burry Port and Ferryside. Further west, manual boxes remain in use at Carmarthen Junction, Whitland and Clarbeston Road, though sadly without any semaphore interest.

Outposts on Anglesey

So, to begin a whistle-stop tour of the Principality, a logical starting point is the ferry port of Holyhead, a place which seems rather down on its luck, with numerous closed pubs and shops and the spacious railway station facilities serving as a reminder of the time before low cost air travel, when this was Great Britain's most important link with Ireland. While the ferries still run, the days of the *Irish*

Virgin Voyager 221117 stands under the 'white elephant' footbridge at Holyhead on 1 February 2017 as it waits to depart with the 08.55 to London Euston.

67008 propels the 13.05 Holyhead to Manchester Piccadilly service past Valley signal box on 31 January 2017, with DVT 82308 at the head of the four-coach formation.

Mail and of hordes of weary travellers transferring from ship to train seem long gone, despite the convenience of the interchange.

Holyhead station is built in a Y-shape, with platforms 2 and 3 providing the closest connection to the ferries, while platform 1 is closest to the town centre, or would be if the modern and expensive-looking footway above the railway tracks had not been locked out of use, an example of the huge amount invested and wasted in the town, according to a local newsagent. This platform is used by the Virgin Trains services to London Euston, while ATW (now Transport for Wales) services normally use platform 2, with platform 3 not seeming to see regular use, but equipped with a run round loop, so suitable for use by any loco-hauled excursion traffic, such as the steam specials which sometimes run along the North Wales Coast Main Line.

An interesting signalling feature can be seen towards the buffer stops on platform three, where there is a semaphore signal and shunting arm facing the buffer stops. Otherwise, the station is a mixture of mechanical and colour lights, although the home signals on all three platforms are semaphores, with tall signals HD23 protecting platform 3, HD35 platform 1 and a short post with signal HD38 controlling exit from the station's busiest platform, number 2.

The station's substantial 1937 London Midland & Scottish Railway (LMS) signal box stands some 300 yards south of the station and can be seen and photographed from a roundabout at the start of the A55 North Wales Expressway, the major dual carriageway road built at huge expense along the North Wales coast in the 1980s and meaning that road is a major competitor for speed with rail, given the numerous stations along this route. Another good vantage point is from a footbridge some way south of the signal box, from where two colour light signals can be seen protecting access to the station, with a semaphore starter and another semaphore protecting an Arriva depot behind the signal box, both of which

have small shunting arms below the main signal.

Heading south-east from Holyhead, the first of Anglesey's five request stops is at Valley, a small settlement near the huge RAF base of the same name, and the first block post on the main line. Here, a London & North Western Railway (LNWR) designed 1904 signal box stands at the south end of the up platform, controlling a level crossing and sidings to the south of the station which form a triangle and, having originally been installed to provide a means of exporting spent fuel rods from the island's Wylfa nuclear power plant in 1962, have more recently found use for turning steam locomotives operating special services to Holyhead.

This is the first of numerous boxes along this line which are Grade II listed; in this case its principal features are its timber cladding, large sash windows, slate roof and an original lever frame in the box itself. Sadly, the box only appears to control two semaphore signals, an up outer home signal not visible from the station and an up home, VY23, standing on the

platform between the signal box and the neglected and boarded up station building. Valley was one of many stations on this route to have succumbed to Beeching and was closed on 14 February 1966 but was thankfully re-opened after 16 years of closure in March 1982.

Continuing in a south-easterly direction and passing another request stop at Rhosneigr, the next outpost of mechanical signalling is at the remote halt of Ty Croes, a wild and desolate place on a wet January morning, where the main sights to see are sheep and the base of a former windmill. The signal box here is older still than the one at Valley, dating back to 1872, and once again Grade II listed. It controls a level crossing between the split platforms, but being only a gate box, not a block post, only two semaphores are visible, both protecting the crossing, TC5 in the up direction and TC2 on the down (Holyhead-bound) line.

What makes Ty Croes architecturally significant is that there is a single storey extension on the south-east side of the box that once served as a booking office

ATW 150258 passes the historic signal box at Ty Croes and is about to make a request stop at the station on 31 January 2017 with the 12.32 Holyhead-Maesteg.

and waiting room – facilities long since dispensed with. In the citation for its listing, it is described as 'a well-preserved example of one of the signal-box and station ranges built to serve the Anglesey section of the Chester to Holyhead railway with a well-composed design, enhanced by decorative brickwork detailing, and original name plates.' It also has the distinction of being one of the oldest working signal boxes still in use in Great Britain.

One final outpost of mechanical signalling on Anglesey can be found at Gaerwen, once a junction for the branch line to Amlwch, which survived for freight traffic long after it lost its passenger service in 1964 and is now the focus of attempts at a potential re-opening. Gaerwen station only outlived the branch line's closure by a couple of years, succumbing like Valley and many others on 14 February 1966, yet remaining a block post and controls an adjacent level crossing to this day.

Gaerwen station was south of the village it served, which stands on Thomas Telford's famous A5 trunk road that has now been superseded by the A55 dual carriageway passing slightly to the north of the village. It is a rather awkward spot to reach, but for those without their own transport, Arriva's 4A Bangor-Llangefni bus gets you there roughly hourly from nearby Llanfairpwll (Llanfair PG) station in less than ten minutes. Once there, the interesting (and unique) feature to note is the post box built into the side of the signal box! Gaerwen box controls four working semaphore arms, two in each direction, but all are at some distance from the box itself and there are rather limited photographic opportunities here.

Passing on a train from Holyhead the day after my visit by bus, gave the chance to spot another surviving semaphore. This is the one protecting the 'mothballed' Amlwch branch, from which the main line connection has been removed, although the heavily overgrown track remains in situ and the signal itself is now surrounded by some mature looking trees!

There are attractive and very historic signal boxes to note at both Llanfair PG – only a gate box – and at Bangor, with more modern structures at both Penmaenmawr and Llandudno Junction, but none of these has any remaining semaphore signalling interest. For the next chance to see working semaphores, we must take a slight diversion up the three-mile long branch line from Llandudno Junction to Llandudno, where colour lights give way to manual signalling from the intermediate station of Deganwy to the charming coastal terminus at Llandudno.

Branch lines from Llandudno Junction

Deganwy is a delightful request stop mid-way and just minutes from both Llandudno Junction and Llandudno, with an attractive LNW-designed signal box dating from 1914 standing at the north end of the down platform. It controls an adjacent level crossing, which is protected in the down direction by a semaphore immediately in front of the box itself and easily photographed from the lengthy up platform.

The up (southbound) starter is a colour light, but the box here has two further semaphores under its control, an up home signal, located quite some distance north of the station and a rarity in the form of a motor-worked up distant signal (DY5), standing between the two golf courses – the North Wales and Llandudno Clubs – which line the route between here and the outskirts of Llandudno. To get photos of these two signals, follow the road over the level crossing and continue northwards on the coastal path from where the footbridge is clearly visible and provides a good vantage point to see these two signals, as well as the Llandudno distant, once a signal arm, but now a board with an image of a distant arm on it.

ATW 150231 departs Deganwy on 1 February 2017 with the 12.33 from Llandudno Junction to Llandudno.

With the slopes of Great Orme and the town of Llandudno in the background, ATW 175106 has just passed the Deganwy up distant with the 14.40 Llandudno-Manchester Piccadilly on 2 February 2017.

There are golf courses on each side of the line as ATW 175108 passes Llandudno's outer home signal on 2 February 2017 with the 14.28 from Llandudno Junction.

Three minutes after pausing at Deganwy, trains reach their destination at Llandudno, a three-platform terminus where most trains only appear to dwell for a matter of minutes before returning back towards Llandudno Junction. This was once a major seaside destination and, while the station has been scaled back from its heyday, there are still some seldom used, but recently re-laid, carriage sidings immediately south of the large and attractive signal box, another LNWR structure, this one dating from 1891 and the subject of a refurbishment in 2004.

Llandudno's former No. 2 signal box controls a gantry spanning platforms 1 and 2, with a separate signal protecting platform 3 with each of the three main arms having a separate shunting arm to control access to the carriage sidings. Besides this trio of signals at the station itself, the box also controls a home signal, outer home and an advanced starter signal on the up line, all of which

can be seen and photographed from a road over-bridge carrying the A546 Bryniau Road, which stands just over half a mile south of the station and offers an excellent view of trains passing the golf courses, with a scenic mountain backdrop. The home signal has an illuminated box below the signal arm which shows which platform the trains are about to enter.

The branch line to Llandudno is not the only place to find semaphore signalling in this area. Head south along the delightful Conwy Valley line to Blaenau Ffestiniog and the one and only passing place on this 28-mile branch line is at what is now called Llanrwst North, having been known as Llanrwst until a new station was opened in 1989 that is somewhat closer to the town. Here, at what is now only a request stop, the signal box controls a passing loop and a home and starting signal in each direction. While no trains are currently scheduled to cross here, both platforms remain in

use and the box's survival means that occasional special trains can be run to Blaenau Ffestiniog without disrupting the timetabled service.

Breaking for the border

Returning to the main line, the next outpost of mechanical signalling was to be found at Abergele & Pensarn, around 15 minutes travelling time from Llandudno Junction and a stop omitted by many services on the North Wales Main Line. It is also a station that has undergone recent change, with the down-side platform relocated to serve what had previously been one of the two fast lines through the station but had survived as a fast line avoiding the platform until its replacement in March 2017. The signal box here is yet another Grade II listed structure, standing between the former fast lines at the east end of the station.

This attractive 1902 LNWR box appears to control four semaphore arms, the junction arm on the down home signal having recently been removed, along with a down starter from the former loop, as part of the platform re-siting following elimination of the loop. Those remaining were home and starter signals in each direction, with those at the western end of the station being close to the platform ends, but those at the eastern end being some 300 yards distant, and beyond a footbridge connecting a mobile home park with the sea-side. This makes an excellent vantage point for photographing trains running on a long straight stretch of line between here and Rhyl.

Next up on our journey towards England is the impressive station at Rhyl, a hugely important holiday resort until well after the Second World War, but another place now reflecting its status of times long past. There can be no better illustration of this than the two magnificent Grade II listed signal boxes at each end of the station, with the No. 2 box at the west end of the station now sadly boarded up, but Rhyl No. 1 Box

ATW 150283 leaves the Conwy Valley Line's only passing loop at Llanrwst North on 23 April 2016 with a service from Blaenau Ffestiniog to Llandudno.

EWS-liveried 67008 approaches Abergele & Pensarn station on 1 February 2017 with the 09.50 Manchester Piccadilly-Holyhead. The down station loop had just been removed along with the junction signal arm, formerly on the post in the foreground.

The North Wales holiday resort of Rhyl can be seen in the distance as ATW 175001 passes Abergele & Pensarn's up starter with the 10.40 Holyhead-Cardiff Central.

EWS-liveried 67008 departs Rhyl on 2 February 2017 with the delayed ATW 09.50 Manchester Piccadilly-Holyhead. Note the down fast line here, which currently sees use by just one train a day.

ATW 150230 passes the Rhyl up home and approaches the attractive Rhyl No. 1 Signal Box on 2 February 2017 with the 11.44 Llandudno-Manchester Airport.

at the eastern end of the up platform very much still alive at the time of my February 2017 visit, albeit with rather fewer working levers than in days gone by.

There is a reminder of how important the North Wales Coast Main Line used to be in the survival of the down fast line through the station. Much of this route was quadruple track from Chester as far as Llandudno Junction, but with the removal of the loop at Abergele this looks to me like the last reminder of that glorious past and, with only one passenger train a day scheduled to pass through non-stop and no regular freight traffic remaining, one wonders how long it will last.

Rhyl No 1 Box controls signals in both directions, as well as a starter signal on the down fast line, while there is a starter in the up direction, not visible from the station, and a down home signal. From a photographic point of view, there is a great shot of the No. 1 signal box and up starter signal to be had from the eastern end of the down platform, while a footbridge just west of the station gives a great vantage point to photograph westbound departures.

Last of the currently open stations on the North Wales Main Line to retain manual signalling was Prestatyn, where an island platform has been retained in the former four-track formation, with the attractive 1897 LNWR signal box standing at the western end of the former down slow platform. Four semaphore arms can be seen from the station, with the up starter being the closest to the platform, while looking further east, the down home signal stands in front of a footbridge some 400 yards distant, with a down advanced starter visible just beyond. In the down (westbound) direction, a starter signal is visible, again at some distance from the platform, at a point where the line makes a right hand bend. What is sadly not visible from the platform, and which I only spotted when passing at speed on my return journey, is an up (working) distant signal (PN14), only the second I noted in North Wales (having missed one at Ty Croes).

Finally, there was a trio of surviving boxes that are not at stations currently open, so places the rail-borne traveller could only glimpse them in passing. First up of these is Talacre, a 1903 LNWR box located on the north side of the line to the east of the former station, another of those to have succumbed in February 1966. Next to be passed on an eastward journey is the 1902-vintage box at Mostyn, another 1966 station closure, but also a Grade II listed structure, along with a former goods shed here. Thirdly, Holywell Junction was another box dating from 1902, standing between the two remaining running lines and which, like Mostyn, shares a Grade II listing with its privately-owned former station building, also closed in February 1966.

Penyffordd and Gobowen

Leaving the North Wales Main Line at Shotton (Low Level) – a station also closed in 1966 but re-opened six years later – the quest for semaphore signals now takes me to two interesting locations on the route southwards from here towards Wrexham and then onwards and past the UK's finest remaining manual signalling outpost at Shrewsbury (featured in the West Midlands chapter). Stepping up to the high level platforms at Shotton, my next port of call is the one remaining location on the quaint 27½-mile long Bidston to Wrexham Central branch line to retain manual signalling, Penyffordd.

Penyffordd is a quiet and rural station located mid-way between Shotton and Wrexham and served by the hourly Class 150-operated trains on this route. Its signal box is the most modern of all the manual boxes remaining in North Wales, a 1972 British Railways (London Midland Region) design and the only one of its type in Wales. The box appears to control six semaphore arms, with outer home, home and starter signals in each direction, although the down (northbound) starter is some considerable distance from the station. There are good shots to be had here looking south, where the up starter stands alongside the down home, while looking north up a long straight stretch of line you can see the down starter, up outer home and up home signals.

ATW 150242 has just left Penyffordd with the 11.49 from Wrexham Central-Bidston. Note the remarkable gradient ahead of the train.

ATW 175107 passes Gobowen's motor-worked down home with the 13.44 departure for Holyhead. Signals in this direction are all upper quadrant, while those on the up line, including the home signal just beyond the signal box, are GWR lower quadrant.

Carrying on down the branch line and connecting at Wrexham General (surely the last former GWR station to have this suffix?) another 20-minute trip south brings you to the charming and historic station at Gobowen, junction for the branch line to Oswestry, whose bay platform remains intact and seemingly ready for use. Gobowen shares a distinction with Yeovil Pen Mill of having lower quadrant semaphores in the up direction and upper quadrant signals in the down direction. The four remaining arms here – all to the north of the station – are controlled by Gobowen North signal box, which stands adjacent to a level crossing immediately north of the up (southbound platform). Besides the fine

station architecture and excellent cafe, an interesting feature to note is that the down home (GN4) is motor worked, despite its proximity to the signal box, and seems to move in a much smoother way than a mechanically-worked signal.

Shrewsbury-Abergavenny

While the incidence of semaphores on the North Wales coast is patchy, the same cannot be said of the Marches route south from Shrewsbury towards Newport, where there are a succession of very varied signal boxes and some pleasantly photogenic locations at which to capture the passing scene. A visit to a number of the surviving boxes in September 2016 began at the oldest surviving box along the route, Marsh Brook, some five miles north of Craven Arms and only just off the A49 trunk road. Here the 1872-vintage box stands alongside the even older former station building, dating back to 1852, with the box controlling a level crossing, protected by single semaphores in each direction.

Mid-way between Marsh Brook and Shrewsbury stands another historic box, dating back to 1872. This is Dorrington, a larger version of the LNW/GWR design at Marsh Brook, where the most interesting feature to note from the nearby road bridge is that the northbound home signal is upper quadrant, while the following

section signal remains a traditional GW lower quadrant, as do the southbound signals.

Craven Arms Crossing was once one of two boxes controlling this important junction with the Heart of Wales line, which branches off immediately to the south of the station. With the station box now long since having disappeared, Heart of Wales line services pause at the signal box to pick up the single line token for the section to Knighton, before crossing to the northbound line just outside the station. The surviving signal box has been likened to a prison, being the product of a re-cladding of an older structure to leave something that is rather less than photogenic!

Oldest of all the remaining boxes on the Marches route south of Shrewsbury is Marsh Brook, five miles north of Craven Arms, which dates from 1872.

The curious looking signal box at Craven Arms Crossing can be glimpsed in the background as ATW 150284 crosses onto the down line on 24 September 2016 and will head onto the Heart of Wales Line just south of the station platforms.

Like many other locations on this route, Craven Arms boasts a goods loop – in this case on the southbound side of the line and just north of the signal box. The station itself is nothing more than a couple of 'bus shelter' type constructions, but the footbridge on the station offers an excellent vantage point to see the array of semaphores between the station and signal box/level crossing, while looking south there is the Heart of Wales line junction alongside the southbound starter (CA17) and, slightly further away, the northbound outer home signal.

Heading south from Craven Arms by road, the small signal box at Onibury,

controlling a level crossing on the busy A49 trunk road, only has colour light signals, but the next semaphores are close by, at Bromfield, a former station that stands adjacent to Ludlow race-course and only a couple of miles north of the town itself. This is a rather more attractive box than Craven Arms, dating back to 1873 and is on the site of a 1958-closed station. There are decent shots to be had here looking in each direction, with the view south being where the line runs close to race-course buildings, with semaphores visible on both the north and southbound lines.

Continuing southwards and only five miles beyond Ludlow, stands Woofferton

Junction, once served by trains to Tenbury Wells and Bewdley, but closed as a passenger station when services on the section west of Tenbury Wells were withdrawn in July 1961. This is another wonderfully attractive spot to appreciate a traditional array of lower quadrant semaphores, with the best vantage point being from a road bridge carrying the B4362 road over the railway line, just a short distance from the A49 trunk road.

Leominster boasts another historic signal box, this time an LNW/GWR design dating from 1875 and situated some distance south of the station, but easily viewed and photographed from an adjacent footbridge. There are no semaphores here in the down (northbound) direction, but two semaphores in the up direction, with a home (LE28) standing on the station side of the footbridge adjacent to the box and a starter (LE27) some 300 yards beyond, at a point where the railway line runs parallel to the A49 trunk road.

Eight miles on from Leominster, the next box, and one with mechanical signalling is Moreton-on-Lugg, site of a significant and fatal signalling incident in January 2010, when a signaller, distracted by a phone conversation, lifted the level crossing barriers, without realising that a train had not yet passed. This is another place at the site of a former station (closed in 1958), where the box controls the crossing and where there is another single goods loop, in this case on the northbound side of the line to the north of the crossing and signal box.

No mechanical signalling survives in the Hereford area, but there are three more manual boxes controlling semaphore signals on this route to the south of the cathedral city, first of which is Tram Inn, just 6¾ miles down the line. Here, the signal box stands opposite an old station building and protects a level crossing on the B4348 road, not far from the village of Didley. While lineside vegetation makes taking a decent picture tricky here,

ATW 175011 passes the Craven Arms up starter on 24 September 2016 with a Cardiff-bound service. Note the Heart of Wales Line diverging to the right.

ATW 175105 passes Ludlow Racecourse and approaches Bromfield Signal Box on 24 September 2016 with a northbound service.

Woofferton Junction is one of numerous signal boxes on the Marches line dating from the 1870s and was a one-time junction for Tenbury Wells and Bewdley. On 24 September 2016 ATW 175001 passes the former station site with a southbound service.

On a gloomy winter's day (12 February 2017) ATW 175116 passes Leominster's 1875-vintage signal box with the 10.31 Manchester Piccadilly-Milford Haven, only running as far as Port Talbot Parkway, due to Sunday engineering work.

One of the more recent signal boxes on the Marches line is this 1943 Great Western Railway design at Moreton-on-Lugg. Like many other boxes, its traditional appearance has been ruined by replacement of its traditional windows with modern single panes.

ATW 175002 approaches Tram Inn, a few miles south of Hereford, with a Llanelli-bound service on 10 February 2017.

I was fortunate to get a nice shot of a southbound train, with home, outer home and northbound starter all visible, by standing on a step ladder kindly lent to me by an ex-railwayman (a fireman) who now runs the large car dealership that occupies the former goods yard site!

Continuing southwards for another 5¾ miles brings you to the highly photogenic location of Pontrilas, where the signal box stands just 200 yards to the north of the former station. This one-time junction for the Golden Valley Railway to Hay-on-Wye is now a delightful bed & breakfast business, which has been in the hands of enthusiasts John Pring and Jo Russell since 1990. Immediately south of the station is the short Pontrilas tunnel, with a good vantage point of the station area from the station garden and from a path off the road passing over the tunnel.

Having spent a couple of nights in the old station (it closed in June 1958), I can highly recommend it for the panoramic view looking north to the signal box, alongside which is a bracket with a home signal and signal for a goods loop, with a southbound home signal nearby. Looking south, there is a southbound starter to the right of the line, immediately in front of the tunnel, while further south an outer home signal can be seen (though not easily photographed) from a bridge carrying the B4347 road over the line.

From Pontrilas, the last signal box controlling working semaphore arms on the Marches route is at Abergavenny, located some 200 yards south of the delightfully restored station and standing on the east side of the line, facing a refuge siding on the southbound side and a goods loop on the northbound side of the line. As at Craven Arms, the best location for photographs featuring the signals here seems to be from the station footbridge, which stands at the south end of the station and looks out to the south on a section of straight track approaching the station past the signal box and goods sidings/loop. In the opposite direction there is a good view of the starter (AY5) at the end of the long northbound platform,

A brief moment of winter sunshine as ATW 175003 passes Pontrilas Signal Box on 10 February 2017 while working the 13.02 Carmarthen-Manchester Piccadilly.

Looking south from the former station platform at Pontrilas (now a recommended bed & breakfast) ATW 175008 approaches the short Pontrilas Tunnel on 11 February 2017 with the 09.00 Carmarthen-Manchester Piccadilly.

ATW 150253 approaches Abergavenny on 25 September 2016, and passes the 1934 GWR signal box, with a service for Manchester Piccadilly.

EWS-liveried 66012 approaches Abergavenny station on 25 January 2017 with a southbound Lafarge aggregates train.

after which the lines sweep away in a right hand curve.

One final mechanical signal box on the Marches Line is its remotest of all. This is Little Mill Junction, 7½ miles south of Abergavenny and at one time the junction of a line which branched off east to Usk, closed to passengers in 1955 but remaining in situ and technically 'mothballed' as far as a military complex at Glascoed just under two miles away. Traffic on the line ceased in 1993 and the remaining line is heavily overgrown, but at the junction, it remains protected by Little Mill's only surviving semaphore signal.

Newport (Park Junction)

When the final stage of the Newport MAS scheme was commissioned in May 1963, it left one solitary outpost of mechanical signalling untouched, possibly because passenger services had been withdrawn the previous year. This was Park Junction, a large 1885-vintage Great Western Railway box on the outskirts of Newport, whose 100-lever signalling frame is a reminder of the intense level of freight traffic that once travelled down towards Newport Docks from Ebbw Vale and the steel works and coal mines that once lined this 20-mile long route.

Park Junction stands at the western point of a triangle of lines which diverge from the South Wales Main Line to the south of Newport station, with Gaer Junction giving trains to and from the Ebbw Vale branch direct access to Newport, while further south is Ebbw Junction from where the current Cardiff-Ebbw Vale passenger service leaves the

Winter sunshine at Park Junction near Newport on 25 January 2017 as ATW 150252 passes the large signal box with a Cardiff Central-Ebbw Vale service.

main line before heading west to Park Junction and on up the valley towards Ebbw Vale. To the west of Park Junction is the remaining stub of a long-closed line to Caerphilly that remains as a freight-only branch line as far as Machen Quarry.

Passenger services were restored to the Ebbw Vale line in 2008, six years after closure of the town's steelworks, and such has been their success that a £40 million upgrading programme is under way to extend sections of double track along the route in order to allow for a much-needed increase in service frequency from hourly to half-hourly. Whether Park Junction signal box survives long enough to ever signal the enhanced service remains to be seen, with its days numbered and replacement now scheduled during CP6 (2019-24).

For the moment, however, it remains an attractive, though difficult, photo spot. There is one good vantage point through some railings on a footbridge which crosses the line just east of the signal box and can be reached by leaving the main Cardiff Road (numerous bus services from Newport Bus Station), walking up Park Avenue and turning right into St. David's Crescent, where the path begins. This gives you a good view of the junction in front of the signal boxes with semaphore arms controlling each direction and a two-arm bracket visible in the distance. Getting a front-on shot of the box itself is possible from the garden of a house in nearby Wells Close, but sadly on the day of my January 2017 visit the house-owner declined my polite request for a moment's access.

Tondu

Like Park Junction, the signal box at Tondu, once known as Tondu Middle, long out-lived passenger services on what had been truncated to become a branch line from Bridgend on the South Wales Main Line to Cymmer Afan – which ceased in 1970 – in order to control the once heavy freight traffic. While that traffic has since disappeared, the box found a new lease of life as the sole signalling on another of the successful re-openings in South Wales, in this case the eight-mile branch line from Bridgend to Maesteg, re-opened to passengers in 1992, four years after the last freight services had finished.

Approaching Tondu on a service from Bridgend the first thing to notice, after an outer home signal located shortly beyond the previous station at Sarn, is a tall two-arm junction signal at the north end of the station's single platform, with the left-hand arm signalling the route onwards to Maesteg and the right-hand one protecting the now-closed freight route to Blaengarw. This line has not seen regular freight traffic since a brief revival 20 years ago (1995-97), but retains a number of semaphore signals, is largely intact, and is the target of eventual re-opening by a group known as the Garw Valley Railway.

Tondu signal box stands to the west of the Maesteg line, just beyond Tondu station, at the point where the Garw line diverges and just beyond a route coming in from the west. This is a diversionary route, which diverges from the South Wales Main Line at Margam and provides an alternative route between Port Talbot and Bridgend when that section of the main line is blocked for engineering work.

It is unclear what the future holds for this route, which requires any train using it to reverse at Tondu, but it was identified by Network Rail in a strategy document heralding the arrival of the InterCity Express Programme (IEP), which stated, 'The section of route between Tondu and Margam will be signalled to passenger standards and a suitable facility to reverse the train at Tondu incorporated into the Port Talbot/Tondu resignalling works.'

The GWR 1883, 65-lever box at Tondu had been destined to be replaced in 2015 and is now scheduled to be replaced during CP6 (2019-24). For the moment it continues to provide a block post and passing point on the Maesteg branch, although with only an hourly service currently timetabled, the passing loop to the north of the station sees no regular use.

A view from the footbridge at Tondu station showing a former platform and signalling on the little-used diversionary route to Margam.

The driver of ATW 150284 is about to give up the single-line token for the section of line to Maesteg as the train approaches Tondu station on 18 April 2016 with a service for Cheltenham Spa.

Almost 80 miles after passing the previous semaphore signals at Craven Arms, ATW 150281 passes Pantyfynnon's southbound home signal on 18 April 2016 with a Shrewsbury-Swansea service.

A footbridge over the line gives a fine view of the signal box and Garw line junction in one direction, while turning to face south there is the remains of a former platform on the Margam route, with a two signal bracket protecting the junction in front of the signal box, starter and advanced starter signals being visible in the southbound direction. Extensive sidings here have long since succumbed to nature.

Pantyfynnon

Catch a Heart of Wales line train south from the manual signalling outpost at

Craven Arms (featured above) and after around two hours and forty minutes, or 78¼ miles of radio-signalled railway, you will find yourself at another oasis of semaphores. This is when you pause at the impressive Grade II listed Pantyfynnon station in Carmarthenshire, along with its nearby, and also Grade II listed, signal box, once known as Pantyfynnon South and now overseeing the entire section from Craven Arms of Wales' most scenic railway line.

There is a total of six semaphore arms at this tranquil location. Immediately to the north of the one remaining platform face there are signals in each direction protecting a level crossing, while at the

south end of the platform, a home signal stands in front of the signal box, while just beyond is a bracket with two home signal arms, one for the main line and one for the freight-only Amman Valley branch, which lost its passenger services in 1958 and closed to freight traffic in 1988, but was revived in 2006 to allow coal trains to run from an open-cast mine at Gwaun-Cae-Gurwen. Further south there is an outer home signal, with a colour light section signal also visible.

Besides its mechanical signals, Pantyfynnon oversees the Heart of Wales Line northwards to Craven Arms by means of a token system called No Signalman Token Remote (NSTR), by which train drivers take a token for each of the route's five sections and at each of the section ends (passing loops) will open a cupboard on the station platform and exchange one token for another one covering the next section of line. So at Pantyfynnon a southbound train will draw forward from the station platform and the driver will surrender a token for the

section from Llandeilo, the southernmost of the five NSTR sections on the route.

Pembrey & Burry Port

In marked contrast to the North Wales Coast Main Line and the Marches Line, just two outposts of mechanical signalling remain along the entire length of the Great Western Main Line in South Wales. The first of this duo is the impressive 1907 GWR box that stands some 400 yards east of Pembrey & Burry Port station. Its substantial size is a reminder of the heavy freight traffic that once originated at countless places like this right across South Wales.

Today, freight has all but disappeared west of Port Talbot, with the exception of limited oil traffic still originating at Milford Haven, and Pembrey box now only seems to control five semaphore arms, along with the adjacent level crossing. Those remaining signals in the down direction are a home, which protects the

Pantyfynnon Signal Box controls both manual signalling, as well as radio signalling, along the Heart of Wales Line. On 18 April 2016 the driver of ATW 150281 pauses to hand over the single line token for the section of line from Llandeilo.

On a wet and gloomy afternoon in South Wales, ATW 175113 approaches Pembrey & Burry Port at 14.02 on 22 February 2017 with the 09.30 Manchester Piccadilly-Carmarthen.

crossing, a starter and an advance starter with a white sighting board behind, which stands beyond a road bridge north of the station.

Looking in the up direction, outer home signal PY82 stands at the end of platform 1 with a home signal close to the signal box and protecting the level crossing. Photography is fairly easy here, with a footbridge just east of the station offering a good vantage point from which to see the station in one direction and the signal box in the other. Besides being a rare outpost of manual signalling, Pembrey & Burry Port station has one other distinction for enthusiasts, as a privately-run ticket office in a wooden cabin close to the up platform was

the last place on the national rail network to sell Edmondson card railway tickets!

Ferryside

Another twelve minutes down the line, and a request to the guard for the train to stop, brings you to the charming station of Ferryside, 296¾ rail miles from the start of this tour of the Principality in Holyhead and home to the last working semaphores to be found in West Wales. Like nearby Pembrey & Burry Port, the rather smaller 1880s vintage box here – standing at the south end of the down platform – also seems to control five semaphore arms, with

a down home protecting a level crossing at the south end of the station and starter and advanced starters visible from the north end of the platform as the line traces a slight S-bend in the Carmarthen direction.

In the up direction, an outer home signal can also be seen from the north end of the up platform, with a home at the opposite end of the platform, facing the signal box and next to a footbridge over the line. This is a pleasantly photogenic spot, with great vantage points for photos in both directions, but particularly to the south from the footbridge where you can watch trains passing along the estuary as they approach the down home signal.

ATW single car 153367 speeds through Ferryside on 22 February 2017 with the 11.09 Pembroke Dock-Swansea.

CHAPTER 5

THE MIDLANDS

Mechanical signalling has largely disappeared across the Midlands region, as it has in the south of England, but there are five areas where it survives, although the first of these has been slated for early replacement. This is a section of the busy cross country route in the East Midlands from Leicester to Peterborough, where six boxes with mechanical signalling have survived between Melton Mowbray, of pork pie fame, and Ketton, a village near the historic town of Stamford, which boasts the rarest signal in Great Britain.

Along with the three other remaining signal boxes on this busy cross country route (Frisby, Manton Junction and Uffington) all are scheduled for replacement, as control of the line passes to the East Midlands control centre at Derby.

By far the most interesting survival to the east of this region is on what is known as the Poacher Line, a meandering route from Grantham through Sleaford and Boston to the east coast resort of Skegness. It can boast a dozen signal boxes along the 55½ mile line, of which seven still control mechanical signalling. If that was not enough, there is also the famous Boston Swing Bridge and the unique 'somersault' signal which survives and still works, alongside the bridge.

Elsewhere, the only line with working semaphores in the North Midlands is the North Staffordshire route between Stoke-on-Trent and Derby, whose seven surviving signal boxes includes the country's newest mechanical box at Uttoxeter, only opened in 1981. Finally, there are two notable signalling centres in the West Midlands, which comprise nine boxes in the Worcester area, bounded by Droitwich Spa, Moreton-in-Marsh and Ledbury and last, but by no means least, the finest collection of semaphores to be found anywhere in Britain, controlled by four signal boxes in the Shrewsbury area.

EAST MIDLANDS

Melton Mowbray

Unlike the other locations featured in this chapter, the 20-mile stretch of route from Melton Mowbray to Ketton, near Stamford, requires the use of private transport, as four of the six boxes which still have any mechanical signalling are at locations without stations or easy access by bus. But taking a journey from west to east, there is no problem in reaching Melton Mowbray, as it is served by all the hourly XC Birmingham New Street-Stansted Airport services on this route.

Melton boasts a fine restored station building and a tall impressive signal box slightly to the west of the up (eastbound) platform and behind a goods loop. The only semaphore arm in view is an up home signal just beyond a road over-bridge some 400 yards west of the station. In the down direction, there are up home signals on the main line and at the exit from a down goods loop behind a bridge carrying Burton Street, but both are hidden behind sighting boards. Out of sight from the station is a down starter near the bridge west of the station carrying the B6047 and an up outer home, which can be seen behind a sighting board from the

XC 170519 passes the attractive Melton Station Signal Box on 5 May 2017 with the 14.35 departure for Stansted Airport, as 170636 departs for Birmingham New Street.

A607 road bridge and is just beyond the junction of the Old Dalby test track.

Whissendine

Head south-east out of Melton on the A606 before forking off to the left and you will reach the first of two neighbouring villages, each with its own signal box and trio of surviving mechanical signals. Whissendine box stands at the site of a former station some two miles north of the village it served, and besides its level crossing barriers has just one remaining semaphore. This is on the up line about 200 yards west of the box but cannot easily be photographed due to lineside vegetation and the crossing barriers being set so far back from the line that there is unfortunately no easy way of photographing a train passing the signal.

XC 170398 has just passed the only semaphore at remote Whissendine on 5 May 2017 with a Birmingham New Street-Stansted Airport service.

Ashwell

Returning to the centre of Whissendine village and heading a mile or so east will bring you to another level crossing on the edge of a village, where the 1912 Midland Railway signal box at Ashwell controls this, and another nearby level crossing, and still has two semaphore arms, both in the up direction, with one being a home signal (the station here closed in 1966) and another, the up starter. This second arm can be easily seen and photographed from the second level crossing, on a lane running from Ashwell to the village of Langham.

XC 170519 approaches the second of Ashwell's two semaphore signals – both in the up (eastbound) direction – on 6 May 2017, with a service for Stansted Airport.

The most prominent of semaphore signals at Langham Junction, near Oakham, is this tall and modern structure, with LM4 controlling the main line and LM2 access to the up loop line. Here 170117 passes with a Stansted Airport-bound service on 6 May 2017.

Langham Junction

Little more than a mile south of Ashwell, Langham Junction, a Midland Railway box dating from 1890, stands at the north western end of goods loops on both up and down lines, which extend all the way to Oakham station. In the up direction, a tall and very modern structure houses the Langham up home LM4 and a small junction arm for the up goods loop (LM2) with the motor-worked Oakham distant beneath LM4. In the down direction there are home signals on the main line and the down goods loop, both hidden behind sighting boards. The best picture opportunity here seems to be from a narrow and overgrown path along the south side of the line.

Oakham Level Crossing

Rutland's county town of Oakham, to the south of Langham Junction, boasts another attractively restored railway station and a Grade II listed signal box to the east of the station platforms that is probably best known for the Airfix kit modelled on it. While the box itself is both photogenic and easily photographed, there is limited signalling interest here, with the only

Oakham Level Crossing is a listed signal box, best known for the Airfix model of it. Here 170106 pulls into Oakham station on 6 May 2017 with the 13.19 departure for Birmingham New Street.

remaining mechanical arm being at the exit from an up goods loop, hidden from view behind a sighting board.

Ketton

Last, but by no means least, of the surviving boxes with mechanical signalling is Ketton, a small village three miles west of Stamford, which lost its passenger service on 6 June 1966, the same day as Ashwell. Here, an attractive 1900 Midland Railway box controls a barrier crossing, with its one remaining semaphore being a real gem. This is a unique lower-quadrant Midland Railway signal – a down section signal – standing on the north side of the line some 300 yards west of the box. For the best vantage point, walk along Barrowden Road away from the box until you reach a path

Britain's rarest and finest surviving semaphore is this Midland Railway wooden post and lower quadrant arm at Ketton, near Stamford. On 28 September 2017, XC 170106 passes with a heavily-delayed service from Stansted Airport to Birmingham New Street.

leading to a foot crossing of the line within 100 yards of the signal.

THE POACHER LINE

Over the past few years, there has been a drastic reduction in the amount of manual signalling in Lincolnshire and neighbouring counties, with notable routes lost including Peterborough-Lincoln, Grantham-Nottingham and Newark-Nottingham. But thankfully, one line which remains an outpost of semaphores is that from Grantham to the east coast resort of 'bracing' Skegness, where careful study of the East Midlands Trains timetable gave me the opportunity to see and photograph six of the seven boxes with manual signalling during a two-day visit by rail in March 2017, as well as a priceless chance to see the unique and last surviving 'somersault' signal in use at Boston Dock Swing Bridge.

Ancaster

After reversal at Grantham, the first station passed by one of the East Midlands Trains Class 156 or 158-operated hourly services from Nottingham to Skegness is just outside the small village of Ancaster, mid-way between Grantham and Sleaford. Here, a small and attractive Great Northern Railway box dating from around 1873 stands at the western end of the up platform and oversees an adjacent foot crossing, with a wooden gate on the south side only, at one of the least-used stations on the Skegness line – a sparse service of just four weekday trains in each direction making a rail-borne visit something of a logistical challenge.

Despite the attractive signal box, and an impressive former goods shed and old name boards at the end of each platform, the signalling interest is rather limited here. Looking west, the up starter is a

Heading east on the Poacher Line from Grantham to Skegness, the first sighting of semaphores is at Ancaster, an attractive location with a sparse train service. On 30 March 2017 EMT 156406 passes non-stop with a service for Skegness.

colour light and the down home (AR2) is behind a sighting board. Turning east, the only semaphore in view is the down starter (AR3) – again with sighting board – some 300 yards from the platform end. Slightly closer to the platform is an up home (AR29) on a modern aluminium post, but again out of sight behind a large sighting board. Neither of the other two semaphore arms are visible from the station – these are a down distant (AR1) and an up distant (AR30).

Sleaford

Passing through the important junction of Sleaford, there are fine boxes at either end of the station, Sleaford West and East but, as at March (see East Anglia chapter), the only remaining mechanical signalling interest is a couple of little-used shunting signals, controlled by the west box. These are a disc SW25 on a siding west of the box and a short shunting arm (SW16) immediately east of the box and visible from the station platform.

Heckington

On departure from Sleaford, the route becomes single track immediately east of the main level crossing, but double track resumes 4½ miles later at the delightful Heckington station. Here the Grade II listed signal box stands at the west end of the up platform, close to a huge Grade I listed windmill. It controls wooden crossing gates and appears to have five semaphore signals. Closest of these is up home HN3 on a tall and modern square galvanised steel post

Heckington is one of the most attractive locations on the Poacher Line, with a Grade I listed windmill standing out of view behind the signal box. Here EMT 156413 approaches the station on 30 March 2017 with the 14.59 departure for Skegness.

that looks rather incongruous in this historic setting.

Looking west, the down home (HN14) stands at the end of the single line section from Sleaford with distant HN15 out of sight from the station. The down (eastbound) starter is a colour light, but on the up line are outer home signal HN2 and distant HN1. The 1876-built signal box here earned its listing by being an unspoiled example of a Great Northern Railway Type 1 box, as well as its proximity to the windmill, and this is a delightful and photogenic spot at which to pass an hour between trains, with the bonus of a railway and heritage museum in the former station building on the down platform.

Hubberts Bridge

At the eastern end of the 8¼ mile stretch of double track from Heckington is another little used station, Hubberts Bridge – ten passengers a week, according to recent figures – where, in marked contrast to the historic GNR boxes at Ancaster and Heckington, is a striking British Rail (Eastern Region) box dating from 1961. Besides a busy wooden-gated crossing, the box here controls six semaphores, with distant, home and starter signals in each direction. Down starter HB11 stands at the end of the eastbound platform, just before the start of the next single line section to Boston, with up home HB24

Hubberts Bridge, just west of Boston, is another station on this line with an extremely sparse train service. It boasts a remarkably modern signal box, which looks rather incongruous alongside the wooden crossing gates.

nearby. Looking west the up starter (HB23) and down home (HB6) stand some 400 yards down the line with the down distant (HB5) visible beyond.

Boston – West Street Junction

Less than ten minutes after passing Hubberts Bridge, the train bears sharply left as it approaches the historic and fascinating town of Boston, whose principal architectural feature, the 282-foot tall tower of St. Botolph's Parish Church and known locally as the Stump, is impossible to miss. A lengthy passing loop begins at the junction of sidings alongside the Docks branch, which joins from the

right and the train then passes the first of West Street Junction Signal Box's handful of semaphores, an outer home (WS30) followed by home signal WS29 standing in front of the box to the south of a busy level crossing and the spacious station.

Like Heckington, West Street Junction Signal Box is another Grade II listed structure and, having been built in 1874, is the oldest GNR box still in use. Completing the picture of the signals it controls, at the north end of the station, down starter (WS28) and up home (WS20) are both lights and the only semaphore interest is a short and unnumbered signal controlling exit from a couple of sidings to the east of the line. In the up direction, home signal WS21 is an attractive lattice

West Street Junction is a listed box at the south end of Boston Spa station, controlling a busy level crossing and a junction to the Boston Docks branch. On 30 March 2017 EMT 156497 approaches with the 13.15 departure for Skegness.

post at the south end of the platform, with a starter (WS22) just in front of a second level crossing on Broadfield Lane, only 300 yards from the station and at the Docks branch junction.

Boston Swing Bridge

To find the real signalling gem in this remarkable town, take a 15-minute walk from the station to a point just before a busy road bridge over the River Witham and head south down High Street for a quarter of a mile to where it becomes London Road and on to a level crossing, where the 1884-built and Grade II listed Boston Swing Bridge, gives access by rail to the docks over the tidal estuary. Wooden crossing gates on the road are protected by two semaphore signals, which are controlled from the boarded-up octagonal chalet-style Swing Bridge Signal Box.

In the Docks-bound direction this is a tall lattice post standing at a rather perilous angle, but in the westbound direction facing towards West Street Junction is a unique survivor in one of the famous 'somersault' signals that were once a feature of the Skegness line. After a lengthy wait on the day of my March 2017 visit, it was an exciting moment to see the old bridge gradually begin to turn under the control of a signalman on the port side of the river. He then crossed the bridge to lock it into position, using a rotating locking wheel, before returning to do the same on the port side. Finally came the moment I had been waiting for as he unlocked the signal cabin and pulled

Another of Britain's rarest signals is the last surviving 'somersault' signal, on the branch line to Boston Docks. Here Port of Boston shunter 09022 draws ten covered wagons of coiled steel across Boston Swing Bridge on 30 March 2017, which will be going forward to Washwood Heath in Birmingham.

off the ancient somersault signal to allow the port's shunter 09022 to inch across the bridge with its semi-regular load, comprising ten covered wagon loads of steel coil bound for Washwood Heath in Birmingham.

Bellwater Junction

North of Boston, the single line becomes double again at Sibsey and remains so for the remainder of the way to Skegness. Sibsey box controls yet more wooden crossing gates, but only colour light signalling, so the next chance to see semaphores just north of here is at Bellwater Junction, though sadly only from the passing train. Here a GNR box dating from 1913 signalled the junction with a route from Woodhall Junction

to the west until its closure in 1970, but today survives to control another wooden-gated level crossing, as well as a crossover between the two running lines.

Wainfleet

Probably best known as the home of Bateman's Brewery, the last calling point for most trains before Skegness is another place to boast a Grade II listed GNR signal box, this one dating from 1899. Wainfleet box controls the barriers of an adjacent level crossing immediately to the north of the station. Its five semaphore arms comprise distant, home and starter signals in the down (Skegness) direction, with just a distant and home signal on the up line. The down line trio can be seen easily from the up platform, but to the north of the

Wainfleet is probably best known as the home of Bateman's Brewery, but also boasts an attractive signal box. EMT 156470 departs on 29 March 2017 with the 15.42 to Skegness.

station and level crossing the up home is obscured by a sighting board and the line then curves sharply to the left, giving no opportunity to see the up distant.

Skegness

So 55½ miles and around 90 minutes from Grantham, and after passing through a sixth and final little-used halt at Havenhouse – two trains each way daily and less than four passengers a week – we reach the end of the line at Skegness. Here again stands another Grade II listed box, this one a Great Northern Railway (GNR) design dating from 1882, which controls access to the six platforms and three carriage sidings. What makes Skegness so attractive as a seaside terminus is that the track layout serving six platforms remains intact, with semaphore arms and shunting arms or discs still in place and operational for each platform, despite only one seeing regular use.

That means six arms controlling the station exit along with an advanced starter, with distant, outer home and home signals protecting the station approach and a shunting signal protecting exit from the three carriage sidings on the west side of the line to the south of the station throat. Paying an off-season visit in a lightly loaded two-car train it is rather hard to imagine the trainloads of day trippers and holidaymakers from the Midlands and beyond who used to arrive here by rail in times gone by, but reassuring that the

Skegness is home to the finest collection of semaphore signals at any UK seaside terminus, as well as a listed signal box, although the hourly train service means many of its signals see little use. Here EMT 158799 approaches on 29 March 2017 with the 15.00 arrival from Nottingham.

NORTH MIDLANDS

Stoke-on-Trent-Derby

Longton is one of the Potteries' Five Towns and signs of its industrial past are very evident in the station area, which is controlled by Foley Crossing Signal Box. On 25 March 2017 EMT 153319 approaches with the 15.27 for Stoke and Crewe.

station facilities remain operational, if they should ever want to come back.

Just six minutes after leaving Stoke-on-Trent on one of the hourly East Midlands Trains (EMT) Class 153-operated services to Derby comes the first sight of mechanical signalling on the North Staffordshire route at Longton, one of the Five Towns making up the Potteries. Here the heavily fortified Foley Crossing box, 300 yards west of the station, controls the locking mechanism to an adjacent pedestrian crossing of the line and seems to have three semaphore arms under its control – up home and starting signals and a down (westbound) starter just beyond the platform end. Metal grilles across all its windows mean the box is not photogenic, but there is a good view through railings at the crossing of the up home signal, while looking towards the station and a large former pottery complex there is an interesting banner repeater signal for the up starter (FY7), which is round a bend and out of sight to drivers at the platform end.

From Longton, a further 20 minutes on the Derby-bound service takes you past an attractive box at Caverswall, though without any remaining semaphores, and on to the main town on this route,

Longton is one of the Potteries' Five Towns and signs of its industrial past are very evident in the station area, which is controlled by Foley Crossing Signal Box. On 25 March 2017 EMT 153319 approaches with the 15.27 for Stoke and Crewe.

Uttoxeter. Getting decent shots here takes a bit of planning, but there are a number of vantage points to discover. On the western edge of the town, for example, Hockley Road level crossing is controlled remotely by the famous Uttoxeter signal box, which stands out of sight round a left hand bend but is only 400 yards away. Here, there is a wooden fence which it is possible to sit on and photograph up (eastbound) services passing semaphore arms on both lines.

The 1981-built signal box – Britain's very last mechanical signal box – looks of a size to have been built for a time when there was still significant freight traffic in the area and, with my count only reaching eight semaphore arms on the main line, together with a number of shunting signals, its 40-lever frame is rather less than fully-employed.

Uttoxeter Signal Box is not easy to photograph at close quarters, standing next to the A518 town by-pass and at the former Pinfold Street level crossing, now open only to pedestrians. There is a good view of it and nearby signals, however, from the ring road bridge immediately to the west of the station. On the rather spartan station, the only signalling interest is a down outer home (UR2), while east of the station – and out of sight – a motor-worked up starter and down distant stand alongside Uttoxeter racecourse's three furlong marker.

Heading east from Uttoxeter, the next box to pass is Sudbury, where an 1885

Hockley Road Level Crossing is a pleasantly rural spot just west of Uttoxeter. Approaching the crossing on 25 March 2017 is EMT 153383/379 with the 12.58 departure from Uttoxeter for Derby.

Britain's newest mechanical signal box is Uttoxeter, opened in 1981 at the heart of what was once an important industrial area. Here EMT 153384 has just left Uttoxeter station and passed the box with the 13.07 departure for Crewe.

Scropton Crossing is a delightfully rural spot south-east of Uttoxeter. On 25 March 2017 EMT 153319 passes the box and crossing with a Derby-bound service.

North Staffordshire Railway box stands on the south side of the line but sadly has no semaphore interest. Just a mile further on however is another signal box gem. This is the remote Scropton Crossing, another North Staffordshire Railway box, dating from 1884, which controls a lightly used level crossing and has six semaphores under its control. These are an up distant (SN1), up home (SN2) and up section signal (SN3) while there is the same pattern in the down, with SN19 being the distant, SN18 the home and SN17 the section signal. All four home signals can be seen from the crossing itself, but more bends in the line mean the distants are out of sight.

Less than two miles beyond Scropton Crossing comes the route's penultimate outpost of mechanical signalling, Tutbury Crossing, another historic gem, reputedly dating from 1872, making it one of the country's oldest surviving boxes. It controls a busy level crossing at Tutbury & Hatton station, which had closed in 1966, but reopened in 1989 and now seems to do good business. It has staggered platforms, with the down (westbound) platform to the west of the crossing and the up platform east of the box and in front of a huge Nestlé instant coffee manufacturing plant. The box here controls four semaphores, with a distant and home signal in each direction. The two home signals are TY6, a tall signal on the up line standing just in front of the signal box and TY2 on the down line, very modern looking and obscured from view behind a sighting board. Once again, neither distant can be seen from the station and crossing.

WEST MIDLANDS

Droitwich Spa

Since completion of a re-signalling project at Kidderminster in August 2012, the northern limit of mechanical signalling in the Worcester area has been at Droitwich Spa, where a Great Western Railway box dating

The huge Nestlé plant dominates this view of re-opened Tutbury & Hatton station, and the historic Tutbury Crossing Signal Box (1872). EMT 153319 approaches on 25 March 2017 with the 11.56 departure for Crewe.

Droitwich Spa is the junction for routes northwards to Birmingham via Kidderminster (left) and Bromsgrove (right). On 24 March 2017, LM 172218/222 are signalled via Kidderminster with the 12.00 departure for Whitlocks End.

from 1907 stands some distance north of the station, at a fork where the double-track route to Kidderminster and Stourbridge diverges to the west, while a single-track towards Bromsgrove, and a junction there with the main Birmingham-Bristol route, passes to the east of the box. This is a very busy spot, with eight passenger trains passing in an average weekday hour, and there is a marvellous array of semaphores to appreciate, notably the rare centre pivot down outer home signals.

Droitwich Spa station has a lot to savour and, apart from the view of the rare signal pair at the north end of the down platform, there is a great vantage point from a narrow road bridge at the north end of the station where you can see no less than eight separate signal arms, including junction signals for the two routes close to the signal box, with further arms on the left hand route to Kidderminster including an exit signal from the little-used down loop, as well as outer home and junction signals in the up direction, and another arm protecting an up goods loop. There is also a signal protecting the Bromsgrove route and a modern looking up home

signal. To the south of the station the only semaphore is an up advanced starter. For a closer view of the large, sadly nameless, signal box you can walk to the end of the station car park where there is a reasonable vantage point through some high railings.

Worcester

Heading south from Droitwich and the first semaphores you will encounter are a three directional gantry just before the north portal of Rainbow Hill Tunnel. These can just be seen from a nearby park, but getting a decent photo seems impossible from any lineside location. Once out of the tunnel, the triangular layout at Worcester becomes evident as the direct route to the city centre Foregate Street station diverges to the right of Tunnel Junction Signal Box, and the main route continues south past the diesel depot to Shrub Hill station. Shrub Hill has seen a significant rationalisation of track and signalling in recent years, but still retains one of the finest collections of mechanical signals in the country.

This fine array of lower quadrant semaphores at the north end of Worcester Shrub Hill station includes a rare mechanical route indicator below signal SH77. On 24 March 2017, LM 172218/222 depart with the 15.47 to Whitlocks End.

Like nearby Droitwich Spa, Worcester Shrub Hill also has a celebrity signal, SH7, which is seen on the left of this view looking south as GWR 43010/125 depart on 24 March 2017 with the 15.54 to London Paddington.

The northern approach to Shrub Hill is controlled by Tunnel Junction Signal Box, standing immediately south of Rainbow Hill Tunnel in the fork between the two diverging routes, while the station and southern approach are controlled by Shrub Hill Signal Box, located just south of the station on the west side of the line. Like Droitwich, it has a particularly special signal in SH7, the up home signal on platform 2, a platform used principally by the local services to Birmingham as many London and southbound services use the main down platform 1, which is signalled for bi-directional use.

Shrub Hill has very much the air of a station that has seen better days and is likely to become even quieter when the long-awaited Worcestershire Parkway station finally opens a few miles south and just beyond Norton Junction Signal Box, at the point where the Cotswold Line to Oxford and Paddington crosses the Birmingham-Bristol route.

Close to signal SH7 on platform 2, one feature worth visiting is a beautifully restored and unique tiled waiting room – a Grade II listed structure that was restored in 2015. To the south of the station are a handful of signal arms, including an outer home with a fixed distant arm, one of a number of fixed distant arms below home signals in the vicinity. Mid-way along platform 1, another interesting feature is SH80, a large round mechanically-worked calling-on signal, which makes a resounding clunk when being pulled off. To the north of the station a three-directional bracket controls access to Foregate Street, the depot and the route to Droitwich, with two more fixed distants here.

Take a Hereford-bound train from Shrub Hill and, after a three-minute journey round a tight left-hand bend, the single track alignment joins the direct route from Tunnel Junction, which it meets at Rainbow Hill Junction, and remains as two separate lines on the approach to the city centre Foregate Street station, following a rationalisation of the layout some years ago. With the exception of a northbound home on the Tunnel Junction line, all signalling here is controlled by Henwick Signal Box, which stands further down the route towards Great Malvern and Hereford, beyond a bridge taking the line over the River Severn.

To the south of Foregate Street station, two motor-worked down home signals controlled by Henwick Signal Box (HK23 for trains departing platform 1 and HK22 for those from platform 2) stand some distance from the platform end – trains on the Tunnel Hill route that have left platform 2 can only cross onto the down line at a point beyond Henwick Box. Looking back towards Shrub Hill from the northern end of Foregate Street station, alongside the Tunnel Junction-controlled home TJ20 stands alongside a Henwick-controlled starter for the line to Shrub Hill, again with a fixed distant arm below.

Henwick

Henwick Signal Box, which dates from 1875, stands at a level crossing in Henwick Road, just west of the river bridge, but there are no signals within sight of the crossing. Head west to the over-bridge on Corner Road, however, and looking west there is a modern single-aspect light in the down direction (HK21), which is a recent replacement for a semaphore, while in the up direction there is Henwick's other remaining pair of semaphore signals, controlling up services, with junction arm HK4 controlling the crossover to the line into platform 1 at Foregate Street and on to Shrub Hill, while HK2, with a fixed distant below, controls access to platform 2 at Foregate Street and the direct route to Birmingham. A new turn-back siding here on the north side of the line was in the process of being re-laid at the time of my May 2017 visit.

Work to install a new turn-back siding at Henwick, just west of Worcester, has recently begun on 29 May 2017 as LM 170511 passes up home signal HK2 with a service from Hereford to Birmingham New Street.

Newland East

Newland East signal box is another Great Western design, dating from 1900 but, like Henwick, having had its original windows replaced with rather unattractive modern single panes. It controls a level crossing near the village of Leigh Sinton, not far from Malvern Link, and controls four semaphore arms, two on each side of the crossing and with a down home signal standing on the right hand side of the line close to the box. Taking shots at the crossing is limited by the barriers being set back from the line, but there is a reasonable vantage point from a road over-bridge about ¾ mile south of the box, although lineside vegetation obscures any view of the down section signal.

It is a dank and misty day as LM 170512/516 approach Newland East Signal Box on 29 May 2017 with a service from Hereford to Birmingham New Street.

Malvern Wells

While semaphores continue to disappear across the country, it is good to find places where they continue to be installed. Moreton-in-Marsh (see below) is one place to boast a new signal arm, and another such location in the Worcester area is Malvern Wells, where two new signals had just been commissioned at the time of my visit in August 2016.

These were a home signal, just north of the former station (closed April 1965) and a slightly shorter signal alongside it, protecting the exit from a loop that is used as a refuge by services from Birmingham that have terminated at nearby Great Malvern. Here, a Great Western signal box, dating from 1919, stands to the south of the former station, close to the end of the double track from Worcester and the mouth of the 1,567-yard Colwall New Tunnel, which opened in 1926 as replacement for an earlier tunnel under the Malvern Hills.

Ledbury

Emerging from a second lengthy single track tunnel, this time the 1,323-yard long Ledbury Tunnel, the final calling point for trains running towards Hereford is Ledbury, a station which shares with Gobowen and Pembrey & Burry Port the distinction of being home to a privately-run ticket office. Here a GWR box dating from 1885 stands at the north end of the down platform, controlling the only passing place on a single track section of line extending from Malvern Wells signal box to Shelwick Junction, north of Hereford, where the Cotswold Line joins the Marches route from Shrewsbury to Newport. Semaphore interest at Ledbury is limited to just two signals, an up starter (L4) and an advanced starter (L5) standing in the short distance between the end of the up platform and the tunnel mouth.

Ledbury has just two remaining semaphore signals, both in the up direction between the station and the single-track Ledbury Tunnel. On 6 August 2016, LM 170631 approaches the tunnel with a Hereford-Birmingham New Street service.

Norton Junction

Returning to Worcester Shrub Hill and now heading three miles south brings you to Norton Junction, a one-time station (known as Norton Halt when it closed in January 1966) where the single track Cotswold Line towards Evesham and Oxford diverges from the double-track heading towards Abbotswood Junction, where it rejoins the main Birmingham-Bristol route.

Here, the 1908 GWR box can be seen by looking south from a bridge carrying a minor road into the village of Norton, while in the northbound direction one can see milepost 117½, beyond which are a down section signal and, at the time of my original visit in May 2016, a fine junction bracket controlling the two routes in the up (southbound) direction. Sadly, on passing in March 2017, the signal arms

Piecemeal replacement of certain semaphore signals in the Worcester area has seen the removal of this junction signal at Norton Junction, three miles south of Shrub Hill station. On 1 May 2016, GWR 166202 is signalled onto the Cotswold Line with a service for London Paddington.

had been removed and a new single aspect colour light signal (NJ9) had replaced it.

Moreton-in-Marsh

When Network Rail was completing a £67 million project to re-double two sections of the Cotswold Line between Oxford and Worcester in 2011 there was not enough left in the kitty to fully re-signal the two re-doubled stretches of line – 4 miles from Charlbury to Ascott-under-Wychwood and 16 miles of line from Moreton-in-Marsh to Evesham.

So in a remarkable, and very British piece of cost saving, semaphore signals were replaced at Ascott-under-Wychwood and Evesham, while those at Moreton-in-Marsh were not only reprieved, along with the 1883-vintage GWR signal box, but a new semaphore was added at the south end of the down platform, in order to allow terminating trains from London to return, without the need to cross to the up line and reverse back into platform two.

Moreton-in-Marsh is a charming and busy country station, with station signs having translations into Chinese and Japanese characters to reflect its role as a major Cotswolds tourist destination. The small signal box, just to the south of the station on the up (southbound) side

of the line, controls seven semaphore arms – a down starter (MM5), down home and outer home signals, an up starter (MM37), the new up starter on the down side (MM27), an advanced up starter and a smaller arm controlling exit from a siding on the west side of the line.

Photographing the station scene is very straightforward, with a bridge carrying the A44 trunk road just south of the station giving a fine view of the station, signal box and two up starters in one direction – with the down starter also visible at the far end of platform one – and a view south on the straight stretch of line towards the long-closed Adelstrop station (of Edward Thomas' celebrated poem fame), where the remaining signals can be seen. These comprise an up advanced starter (MM37), a down home (MM3), down outer home (MM2) and a signal controlling exit from the downside refuge siding (MM10).

Shrewsbury

For the sheer joy of appreciating mechanical signalling in action, there can surely be no better place in Britain to visit than Shrewsbury. Here, no less than three major signal boxes can be seen from the station platforms; the majority of signalling remains mechanical and there is not only a curious mix of upper and lower quadrant signals, but you will find two extremely rare wooden arms, the likes of which I have only ever seen at Liskeard and Droitwich Spa. To begin an appreciation of what Shrewsbury has to offer, it is worth imagining you are on the station and for me to describe what there is to see from the platform, beginning at the north end of the station, where the routes to Chester and Crewe diverge in front of the impressive Shrewsbury Crewe Junction Signal Box.

The one remaining signal gantry spans from the north end of platform 3 to a point beyond platform 4 but only has

GWR 180102 approaches Moreton-in-Marsh on 21 August 2017 with the 15.22 London Paddington-Great Malvern.

With the magnificent Shrewsbury Severn Bridge Junction Signal Box in the background, ATW 175001 pulls out of platform 4 on 13 May 2017 with the 15.15 departure for Cardiff Central, a service from Holyhead.

The most notable signals at Shrewsbury are this pair (SBJ11) at the south end of platform 7. Here ATW 175003 departs on 13 May 2017 with the 15.40 for Pembroke Dock.

one semaphore arm – a lower quadrant down starter from platform 3. Close by is a home signal CJ3 protecting platform 4. The other eleven semaphore arms in view include a down starter from platform 7, up home signals from the Crewe line controlling access to platforms 7 and 4, two junction signals in the up direction on the line from Chester along with the upper quadrant signal beyond the Chester Road bridge half a mile north of the station, along with a down advanced starter on the Chester route.

For the best view to the north of the station it is well worth taking a ten-minute walk out of town on the A528 Chester Road until you reach a bridge over the line. Looking back towards the station, the closest signal is a down starter, while some distance beyond and just across the running lines from Crewe Junction box are junction signals CJ2 in the up direction, with sighting boards behind each of the two arms, and a further junction pair (CJ6) closer to the station. Looking north from the Chester Road bridge, the one signal in view is an upper quadrant outer home, making a contrast with the other Crewe Junction lower quadrant arms.

Returning to the station and standing at the south end of platforms 6 and 7 beneath the famous pair of centre pivot arms (SBJ11) gives the best impression of all of this remarkable location. There are no less than fifteen semaphore arms in view, together with the big daddy of manual signal boxes, Severn Bridge

Shrewsbury Castle forms the backdrop of this view from the Chester Road bridge as ATW 158834/820 approach Crewe Junction Signal Box on 13 May 2017 with the 12.33 departure from Shrewsbury to Birmingham International.

Junction and the abbey behind it. The 1902 LNWR box has 180 levers and has been the largest mechanical box in the world since the closure in 2011 of the 191-lever box at Spencer Street in Melbourne, Australia. Looking to the left, Abbey Foregate box can be seen, while to the right of the box stands a starter for the Marches Line route and an adjacent signal protecting the western end of the avoiding line at what is called English Bridge Junction.

Having appreciated what the station has to offer, it is now well worth heading south from the station, through the charming town, and over the Severn bridge after which a right turn and short walk down the A5191 brings you to a turn called Betton Road, leading to Sutton Bridge

Junction. Here, the 1913 GWR box stands between a footbridge and a former road bridge, now also for pedestrian use only.

Looking north from the footbridge, you find SUB5 in the up (northbound) direction, and junction arms in the southbound direction, with the left hand arm giving access to the Aberystwyth route, which diverges just south of the road bridge. As elsewhere there is a mixture of upper and lower quadrant signals, with junction signals and the signal off the Mid-Wales route being lower-quadrant, and others upper-quadrant. Sutton Bridge was once a three-way junction, and a red brick bridge immediately behind the box is a reminder of the lost Severn Valley route south to Bridgnorth.

From Sutton Bridge, the route to Shrewsbury's fourth and final remaining manual signal box takes you westwards along Scott Street, then back towards town on the A458 Old Potts Way, where to your left – sadly obscured by lineside vegetation so difficult to photograph – you will see a lower quadrant home signal, controlled by Severn Bridge Junction, with Sutton Bridge's distant below it. After the removal of the junction signal at Norton Junction, near Worcester, in early 2017, as mentioned above, this is now the last working lower quadrant distant signal on the national railway network.

Head on next past the Abbey and take a left turn into Monkmoor Road where you will find an over-bridge with an awkwardly high parapet, just east of Abbey Foregate Signal Box. My opportunity to photograph the panoramic scene from here only came when I persuaded the local newsagent to lend me a stool to stand on! Once standing on the stool there is a fine view of the station's eastern approach, with both Abbey Foregate and Severn Bridge boxes in view and a mass of semaphore arms in the distance, though none being close at hand, with the junction signal in front of Abbey Foregate box being a colour light.

ATW 175102 has just passed Sutton Bridge Junction on 13 May 2017 with a service from Cardiff Central to Holyhead. Note the shunting arm below the distant signal, for access to the goods sidings and lower quadrant arms in the southbound direction.

CHAPTER 6

NORTH-EAST ENGLAND

Significant outposts of mechanical signalling remain across the North East, with what survives being in some fascinating locations in a region that is home to many of the oldest remaining signal boxes on the British rail network. These include the two oldest boxes of all – Norton South and Norton East – dating from 1870, along with a number of boxes between York and Scarborough, which date from the early 1870s. There are some charming locations to savour and photograph, amongst which I would single out Haydon Bridge, Knaresborough, Norton-on-Tees and Prudhoe.

Harrogate-York

For the sheer number and variety of manual signal boxes on a relatively short stretch of line, there must surely be little in Great Britain to match what remains along the 17½-mile section of the York to Harrogate line that extends from Poppleton, a village on the outskirts of York, to the spa town of Harrogate. For the price of an £8.50 day return from York to Harrogate (2017 price), the line is a real treat for lovers of traditional signalling. Here you will see five very different signal boxes at stations, as well as getting passing glimpses of four gate boxes, all controlling crossings protected by semaphore signals and two of which are at the site of former stations (Marston Moor and Hessay).

Starting a return trip to York from Harrogate, the first thing to notice at this large station – principal stop on the horseshoe shaped route from York to Leeds – is how the southern end of the station is all controlled by MAS signalling while semaphores prevail at the northern (York) end of the station. It follows completion of a £16 million re-signalling programme from Kirkstall Viaduct to Harrogate in October 2012. This led to closure of manual signal boxes on that section of the route at Horsforth and Rigton and transferred control to the relatively modern Harrogate signal box, built by the LNER in 1947 and known as Harrogate North until closure of Harrogate South box in 1981, but still identified on its name-board as Harrogate North.

Mixed two, three and four-car formations of Class 150 series units currently provide services on the route. There is some use too, of the reviled 'Pacer' units, although on a weekend visit in January 2017, I only saw one such unit in use. Having survived its proposed closure in the 1963 'Beeching Report' (the line was reprieved in September 1966), a rationalisation in 1972/3 led to a partial singling of the route. Times change, and in 2015, plans to electrify the route and re-double the two sections of single line (Knaresborough-Cattal and Hammerton-Poppleton) were published. However, plans to re-signal the route eastwards from Harrogate to York having slipped from 2018 to at least 2021 (according to one signaller I met), so there seems little prospect of any early go-ahead for wholesale modernisation.

Standing at the north end of Harrogate's York-bound platform, two modern semaphore arms control departure from the station (H57) and the relief line between the two platform tracks (H59), with a separate, and older, signal controlling exit from an adjacent siding, where diesel units stable. Looking out around the right hand curve there is an impressive gantry spanning the

two running lines on which stand the up (Leeds-bound) home signal with a small shunting arm below and another shunting arm protecting the eastbound direction. The gantry looks in need of a coat of paint and has not been enhanced by addition of a modern and unpainted waist-high handrail and steps up from the gantry to the home signal. North of the station area, there are two more semaphore signals, an advanced starter and an outer home.

Four minutes and 2¼ miles north-east of Harrogate is the busy intermediate station of Starbeck, where an attractive two-storey signal box dating from 1915 stands at the eastern end of the Harrogate-bound platform and controls a level crossing at that end of the station. The only signal on the station itself is an eastbound home (SB3) which is a three-aspect colour light, with the only remaining semaphore signal being an eastbound outer home signal, which can be seen and photographed some distance away from the end of the eastbound platform.

Continuing a fascinating journey back towards York and another four-minute, 1½ mile hop brings you to the architectural gem of this route, the Grade II listed station at Knaresborough, sandwiched between an impressive stone viaduct over the River Nidd and a tunnel at the eastern end of the station. Immediately in front of the tunnel on the eastbound side stands a water tower, dating from the line's opening in 1851, while at the other end of the eastbound platform is the unique signal box, opened in 1890 and built onto the end of a row of terraced houses. The box here controls three semaphore signals – a westbound home, standing on a bracket at the end of the eastbound platform, a down home signal at the far end of the viaduct, and a starter in the westbound direction, which is out of sight round a left hand bend beyond the viaduct.

Semaphore signalling survives only at the northern end of Harrogate station. On 7 January 2017, Northern Rail 153317+150204 arrive from York with a Leeds service.

Northern Rail 155344 departs Knaresborough on 7 January 2017 with the 12.36 service to Leeds, passing the unique and listed signal box.

A panoramic view of Knaresborough station from the garden of Carriages Wine Bar on 7 January 2017 shows Northern Rail 150204+153317 with the 13.05 to Leeds.

Knaresborough is the terminus for one of the half-hourly weekday services from Leeds operated on this route, with an hourly service onwards to York. Terminating services arrive in the eastbound platform (2) then use a cross over in front of the signal box to draw onto the viaduct, before entering platform 1 and awaiting a return to Harrogate and Leeds. Services to and from York will pick up or hand over the Key Token for the single track section to Cattal from the Knaresborough signaller, who also controls a busy pedestrian crossing of the line at the west end of the station, which is locked shut when a train is signalled. There are numerous photo spots on the station itself, but for a fabulous view down onto the station scene, I can highly recommend a visit to Carriages Wine Bar, which stands above the tunnel to the east of the station and has a terrace offering a clear view of the station below.

A six-mile stretch of single track eastwards from Knaresborough takes you to the first of three delightful and rural wayside stations, each of which has a level crossing – one with wooden gates – and at each of which there is an exchange of Key Token between driver and signaller and the beginning and end of the route's two single track sections. First of this trio is Cattal, where a diminutive 1892 vintage North Eastern Railway signal box stands at the western end of the York-bound platform, controlling level crossing gates and two semaphore signals – a home signal in the York-bound direction and a westbound starter with both home and distant arms.

Northern Rail 150132/205 head onto the single track section of line at Cattal on 7 January 2017 with the 13.27 to Leeds.

From Cattal, a 1½-mile section of double track takes you to the next of this charming trio, Hammerton. Here, there are wooden crossing gates at the west end of the station, with the signaller based in an office within a station building on the York-bound side of the station, with the signal levers housed in what looks like a large cupboard on the platform itself! The signaller here has three semaphore signals under his control – an eastbound home signal just beyond the wooden crossing gates, and eastbound starter at the end of the platform and a westbound home signal. Another semaphore arm visible from the station platform is a distant signal in the eastbound direction, controlled by the crossing box at Wilstrop, which will only be in the off position when the crossing gates there close to road traffic.

Wilstrop is the first of three gate boxes on the 5¾ mile section of single line from Hammerton to Poppleton, each protected by distant and home semaphore signals controlled by signallers at the separate locations. While Wilstrop was not a passenger station, the other two – Marston Moor and Hessay – are both at the site of former stations. Marston Moor, better known as the site of a famous Civil War battle on 2 July 1644, has a Grade II listed gate box on the station's former eastbound platform, the station having closed to passengers in September 1958. Nearby Hessay suffered the same fate, but 60 years later, the station building survives in private ownership, with the crossing gates

Northern Rail 150273 has just left the short section of double track from Cattal to Hammerton with a service for York and approaches the Marston Moor distant signal.

controlled by a signaller also based on the former up (York-bound) platform.

One final outpost on this route of manual signalling is at Poppleton. This is a station serving a number of villages on the outskirts of York, which faces competition for passengers from a nearby and newly opened 'park and ride' facility on the A59 trunk road. Here the advertised £2.80 return fare to York undercuts the £3.00 cost of a day return on the train (2017 prices) with considerably greater frequency of buses than the hourly rail service.

Like Hammerton, it retains wooden crossing gates, with the signaller housed in a small single-storey wooden box dating from the 1870s (though subsequently extended) which is next to the crossing and across the road from the eastbound platform. The signaller here controls two semaphore arms – a tall home signal just west of the crossing gates and another at the end of the westbound platform. For a panoramic view of the station, I can recommend a ten-minute walk out to a

bridge over the line on the A59, reachable safely on a pavement alongside the trunk road, which offers a pleasing and uninterrupted view of the station and both semaphore signals.

York-Scarborough

Head north-east out of York and you will soon pass a trio of very contrasting manual signal boxes standing on the route to Scarborough within a few miles of each other just west of Malton, each one with a different style of level crossing to operate. First up is Barton Hill, where hand operated lifting barriers are controlled by a wheel in what looks a modern box, but is actually an LNER design from 1936. There are two home signals here, one in the up direction stands adjacent to the box, while beyond the A64 overbridge stands Barton Hill's down home signal.

Little more than a mile further on, Howsham is a delightful small North

Northern Rail 153352/342 approach the end of the single track from Hammerton at Poppleton station on 8 January 2017, with the 14.06 departure for York.

Barton Hill is the first of four locations to retain semaphore signals on the York-Scarborough route. Its 1936 LNER box is seen here on 25 September 2017.

TPE 185119 approaches the modern down home signal at Howsham on 25 September 2017, with the 09.22 Liverpool Lime Street-Scarborough.

A TPE Class 185 has just passed the attractive box and wooden-gated level crossing at Kirkham Abbey on 25 September 2015 with the 11.50 Scarborough-Liverpool Lime Street.

Another set of mechanically-worked wooden level crossing gates survives at Weaverthorpe, the fourth and final location of mechanical signalling between York and Scarborough, as seen on 26 September 2017.

Eastern Railway box dating from 1873, where the signaller operates lightweight metal gates protecting a quiet country lane. It also has two home semaphores, both close to the crossing and, in the down direction, being mounted on one of the modern steel posts.

Third of this trio, and pick of the bunch, is the superbly preserved Kirkham Abbey box, another NER design from 1873 and again controlling barriers across a quiet country lane. Here the wooden gates close mechanically when the signaller turns a large hand-operated wheel in the box, which must be something of a rarity. Mechanical signalling here comprises a down home and up section signals, both visible from the crossing, and an up home around a right hand bend from the box, but visible from a footpath along the north side of the line.

Fourth and last of the remaining semaphore interest between York and Scarborough is another real gem. This is yet another 1873 NER design at Weaverthorpe, a long-closed station on a quiet country lane just north of the village of Sherburn and another place with mechanically-worked wooden crossing gates. Four semaphores remain here, being home and section signals in each direction, with the best vantage point being from the south side of the crossing looking west.

Gilberdyke Junction-Ferriby

Rail-borne visitors to the UK's 2017 city of culture could probably have been forgiven for failing to spot during the latter stages of their journey to Kingston-upon-Hull what many enthusiasts would

Hull Trains 180109 passes Gilberdyke Junction Signal Box on 27 September 2017 with the heavily-delayed 09.48 London King's Cross-Hull.

describe as a stretch of some of the finest remaining semaphore signalling in England. Sadly, however, by the time this book is published the manual signalling between Gilberdyke Junction and Ferriby will have disappeared in a £50 million upgrading project, first announced in February 2016 and completed in November 2018.

A key driver of the re-signalling project was a wish to enable later services at Hull, as the manual signal boxes close overnight. That meant the last train departing Hull at 22.20 and the final arrival of the day, according to the last timetable before re-signalling, a Northern Rail service from York at 23.35. Once re-signalled, the hope locally was for faster trains and potentially for all-night services.

Paying a brief initial visit by rail in January 2017, I was able to spend time photographing at Gilberdyke and Brough but, with Sunday trains not stopping at Broomfleet, I was not able to photograph the box, nor the five other signal boxes

and gate boxes at Oxmardyke, Cave, Crabley Creek, Welton and Melton Lane. Nevertheless, a rather misty Sunday morning gave a good flavour of the remarkable heritage represented by the eight boxes along this 9½-mile stretch of main line, controlling what was reputedly the largest number of semaphore signals remaining on any English main line route.

Gilberdyke lies 17 miles inland from the end of the line at Hull and is a junction where the route towards Goole and Doncaster diverges west of the station from the main route on towards Selby and Leeds. With its once heavy freight traffic the route back towards Brough was previously quadruple track, but was rationalised in 1987, when new platforms were built at Gilberdyke and Broomfleet and signals relocated to stand on the track-bed of the former outer running lines.

Looking west towards the junction from Gilberdyke station, there were two separate home signals standing in the formation of the former platform road,

DB 66053 heads a train load of steel coils from Hull to Masborough onto the Goole route at Gilberdyke Junction on 27 September 2017 and passes 158787 with the 12.52 Doncaster-Hull.

with the junction and signal box visible a short distance away beyond a road over-bridge. From this over-bridge it was possible to get a good view of the 1903 North Eastern Railway (NER) signal box and most of the semaphores it controlled at the junction itself and beyond in the Selby direction, where there were a single arm advanced starter and an outer home signal in the down (eastbound) direction.

Turning in the opposite direction and with a good vantage point from the station footbridge down one of the longest stretches of straight track in Britain, four semaphores were visible. In the down direction, the starter had a home and a distant arm, with the latter worked from the nearby Oxmardyke gate box, which also controlled a home signal protecting the crossing, while in the up direction

there was an outer home, also with a distant arm, and a home signal with a single arm.

Paying a return visit to the area in August 2017, I decided to see as much as I could of the remaining semaphores by taking the one daytime service from Gilberdyke that stops at Broomfleet (11.26) and then walking from Broomfleet to Brough, in order to see the boxes at Cave and Crabley Creek. Finally, on a third visit, in late September 2017, I was finally able to get to the three boxes I had previously missed, including what must be the pick of the bunch from an architectural perspective, the 1901-vintage gate box at Oxmardyke Crossing.

Like Gilberdyke, Broomfleet was the scene of considerable signalling activity at the time of my visit, with a dozen or

GBRf-liveried 66724 passes signalling engineers working at Broomfleet on 9 August 2017 with a service from Hull Coal Terminal to Ferrybridge Power Station.

so men in high-vis jackets working close to the fine 1904 NER box. Semaphore signalling here comprised up and down home signals, with an up starter also visible in the distance, while in the down direction a colour light protected nearby Cave Crossing, with up home and distant signals on a single post visible just beyond that crossing.

Cave was another 1904 NER box, but a diminutive structure compared to Broomfleet, which was the largest of the remaining boxes on this stretch of line. It is only a 20-minute walk along country lanes from Broomfleet and there was a nice vantage point looking east from the north side of the crossing to see the up home and distant signals, while looking west down the dead straight line, Broomfleet station, box and signals are all visible a mere half-mile or so in the distance.

The walk from Cave to Crabley Creek is somewhat more challenging and requires the local Ordnance Survey map to show a path crossing the lane leading away from Broomfleet about 300 yards beyond the crossing. Head south-east along this path and over the railway line, then bear left and make for the range of buildings that make up Crabley Farm. This is a charming spot, where the box controls wooden gates giving access to the farm area, as well as three semaphore arms, home signals in each direction and a motor-operated up distant (the down distant is a light).

Talking to the helpful signaller at Crabley Creek, a curious quirk of railway history means that when the re-signalling project is completed, the box here will have to remain manned, even when control of the route is from the Railway Operating Centre (ROC) at York. That is because a

Northern Rail 158904 approaches the Cave up home signal (with the Broomfleet distant beneath) on 9 August 2017, operating a Bridlington-Sheffield service.

A TPE Class 185 unit passes Crabley Creek on 9 August 2017 with a Manchester Piccadilly-Hull service. The new TPE livery has led to the removal of set numbers from the front of these units, making high speed identification difficult.

deed in the original sale agreement when the line was built, by which the owner of Crabley Farm allowed a level crossing to be built, on condition that it was always manned!

From Crabley Creek to Brough is a steady 2½-mile trek along a rather muddy dyke that forms part of the Trans-Pennine Trail and runs parallel to the railway line, close to the north bank of the River Humber, with the Humber Bridge looming in the distance, beyond the British Aerospace plant at Brough. Walking this rather desolate stretch of path gave you a chance to photograph trains passing Crabley Creek's motor-operated up distant signal.

At Brough, semaphore signalling was rather less evident than at Gilberdyke and other places along this line. There is a tall up starter, while the down and up home signals are both three-aspect colour lights. Take a 300-yard walk down a path alongside the line, however, and you reach a level crossing adjacent to Brough East signal box, yet another 1904 NER design.

There is a good view from the south side of the crossing looking east towards the nearby crossing box at Welton, with three semaphore signals in view, all carrying both home and distant arms. There is another good vantage point from a foot crossing midway between Brough and Welton, reached by a path leading east behind a factory building just to the south of the Brough level crossing.

Returning for my third and final visit in September 2017, I was able to see the final two boxes on this fascinating stretch of line. Welton is a small NER crossing box, also dating from 1904, which oversees a user-worked crossing on a quiet road called Common Lane, and only has four signal levers – home signals in each direction and a pair of motor-worked distant signals.

A mile further east and controlling a crossing on Gibson Lane South in the heart of a busy industrial area was Melton Lane, another attractive NER box, dating from 1921 and standing adjacent to the former

The tall up starter at Brough station can be seen in the distance as Northern Rail 142026 approaches Welton with a Doncaster-Hull working on 9 August 2017, and has just passed 158848 on a Hull-Doncaster service

Northern Rail 158859 approaches Welton Crossing on 27 September 2017 with the 10.11 Bridlington-Sheffield.

Hull Trains 180111 approaches Melton Lane on 27 September 2017 with the 10.30 Hull-London King's Cross.

Melton Halt, which closed in July 1989. Here, the only remaining part of the once quadruple track layout is an up relief line, extending from Ferriby station to the western end of the former Melton station. The route's most easterly semaphore signals are up home and distant signals on the main line, alongside a home signal on the up relief line, while in the down direction, a down home with distant arm below stands on what was the down slow line. There is also an up starting signal (ML9) at the far end of the former station platform, shortly before the end of the relief line.

Hull-Scarborough

Heading north now from Hull, there are only two remaining outposts of mechanical signalling on the Yorkshire Coast Line from Hull to Scarborough, but both are well worth a visit. First up is the magnificent Bridlington South Signal Box, controlling the southern approach to the line's principal intermediate station. Although much rationalised, and with the station reduced from what were once eight platforms to three today, it still controls an array of up home signals, together with a starter and an up section signal, visible in the distance from the nearby A165 road bridge.

In the down direction, the only semaphore is a home signal close to the box, which has a short shunting arm beneath. There is a good view of the signals and the box beyond from the south end of platform 4, the platform used by trains to Scarborough. For an even better view of the box and chance to photograph a departing train, I found a spot behind the large B&Q store opposite the box and stood on one of the store's trolleys, pushed against the fence, to get the shots I wanted!

Bridlington is one of only two locations between Hull and Scarborough to retain semaphore signals. Northern Rail 158909 has just passed the magnificent 1893-vintage Bridlington South Signal Box on 26 September 2017 with a service from Sheffield.

Northern Rail 158853, sporting a colourful new livery, approaches Bridlington South Signal Box on 26 September 2017 with the 13.41 Bridlington-Hull.

In stark contrast to the huge box at Bridlington South, the only other remaining location of semaphores on the Hull-Scarborough route is another of Britain's oldest survivors, the NER 1874-vintage gate box in the village of Gristhorpe, just north of Filey. Gristhorpe Crossing retains hand operated wooden gates and on the opposite site of the quiet lane from the box stands the well-preserved former station (closed February 1959).

Only four signal levers remain operational in what was once an 18-lever frame – these are the up home (6), down home (17) with two shorter yellow levers for the motor worked distant in the up direction (6) and down (18). One unique feature of this charming box is a painting on the end wall of a steam train in Gristhorpe station, dated 1981, the work of a former signaller here, Pete Bartle.

Darlington–Bishop Auckland

The 12-mile branch line from Darlington to Bishop Auckland is a pleasantly rural route, with plenty of railway interest and a limited amount of manual signalling to savour. Shortly after leaving the main station (Bank Top, to give it an historic title) you reach North Road station with its impressive museum buildings and overall roof. Less than ten minutes later there is a complete change of era as a section of overhead electrified line appears on the left, which is a test track for the Intercity Express Programme (IEP) trains being assembled at the Hitachi plant here for use on the East Coast and Great Western Main Lines.

Shortly after this come the staggered platforms of Heighington station, with its 1872-vintage Grade II listed North Eastern Railway signal box controlling the start of the double track section to Shildon. Sadly, mechanical signalling here was replaced in 2014 by single aspect colour lights, but there remains one outpost of mechanical signalling on the route at Shildon, northern end of the double track section.

Here, there are masses of National Railway Museum exhibits to see on approaching the station, along with a

trio of very modern looking semaphore signals. First of these is a down home (S25) while in the up direction starter S31 stands opposite the NRM site, a quarter of a mile from the station, while between the signal box and up platform end is up home S32. Shildon is another North Eastern Railway box, dating from 1887, which controls colour light signalling on the single-track section onwards to Bishop Auckland, including a junction signal on the approach to that station giving access to the preserved Weardale Railway.

Stockton-Billingham

Rivalling Harrogate-York as the finest remaining manual signalling anywhere in the North-East is the 4½-mile section of line between Stockton-on-Tees and Billingham. Travel this line and you will pass the two oldest signal boxes in Britain, both dating from 1870, at Norton South

and Norton East Junctions, along with two other fine survivals at Norton-on-Tees (built 1897) and at Billingham (1904). Three of the four remain in daily use, while the listed Norton East Box is normally 'switched out' as there is no regular traffic on the north side of the triangle from here to Norton West – start of the diversionary Stillington Line to Ferryhill on the ECML – and is boarded-up in order to prevent vandalism.

Visiting the five boxes at Norton and Billingham makes for a fascinating day with a fair bit of walking between the different locations, but all on level roads with pavements. My August 2017 visit began with a train journey to Thornaby, then travel on an Arriva no. 15 bus to Roseworth – the buses run every 8 minutes from a stop near the station and the journey takes about 25 minutes. Alighting at a stop in Ragpath Lane called Kiora Hall, it was a short walk north over Junction Road and up Blakeston Lane to reach the level crossing and Norton West Box.

Northern Rail 142068 passes Shildon Signal Box on 18 May 2017 with the 16.13 departure for Bishop Auckland. This outpost of the National Railway Museum boasts the only remaining semaphore signals on this line.

Britain's oldest main line signal box in daily use is Norton South, just north of Stockton-on-Tees, and seen here from a bridge carrying the B1274 road north of the box.

There is very little traffic on the Stillington Line, and with nothing scheduled on the day of my visit, I quickly pressed on. Returning to Junction Road and heading east brings you to a bridge over the west curve linking Norton West with Norton South. Having also made an unsuccessful detour to a foot crossing some way south of Norton South box, this seems to be the best vantage point from which to see Britain's oldest working box, which stands on the west side of the junction, some 300 yards from the bridge. An up home signal protects the west curve with another just visible on the main route from Sunderland, converging from the left, but signals south of the box are both colour lights.

Setting off from this bridge, it is only a short walk to the joint oldest box, Norton East, by continuing along Junction Road then taking a left turn into Kew Gardens, from where a farm track leads to a crossing close to the box. Being routinely 'switched

out', the boarded-up box is not very photogenic (it is Grade II listed). There is, however, signalling interest here, with home and distant signals on the down main, the north side of the triangle from Norton West and a pair of modern home and distant signals in the up direction controlling the junction.

A brisk 1½-mile walk from here, continuing along Junction Road once again then taking a left turn into Station Road shortly before a junction with the A1037, brings you to the splendid tall box at Norton-on-Tees. There are a number of photo opportunities here, but best of all is the panoramic view from a footbridge standing about 200 yards west of the level crossing. Reaching the final box on this fascinating stretch of line at Billingham is a 1.8-mile walk back to Junction Road then following the A1027 towards Billingham, over a junction with the A19 and another roundabout before taking a left turn into Station Road.

Northern Rail 142068 passes the very modern semaphores protecting Norton East junction on 18 August 2017 with a service from Hexham to Nunthorpe.

Britain's joint oldest signal box, though sadly not in regular use and boarded up for security reasons, is Norton East, seen here on 18 August 2017. It stands less than a mile from the other 1870 box at Norton South.

GBRf-liveried 66763 approaches Norton-on-Tees on 18 August 2017 with a service from Drax Power Station to Tyne Coal Terminal.

DB-liveried 66002 passes the magnificent Norton-on-Tees Signal Box on 18 August 2017 with a train load of empty wagons running from the steelworks at Hartlepool to Tees New Yard.

Billingham is another very impressive and tall North Eastern Railway box standing at the site of a former station – Billingham station has been re-located to a site three-quarters of a mile north-east of its original location. There is only limited semaphore interest visible here, home junction signals in the down direction with B37 controlling the main line and B34 the freight route to Seal Sands. For a good shot of the box, signals and cast iron footbridge, head round the corner into St. David's Close, where there is an excellent vantage point.

Carlisle–Newcastle

Take a trip from Carlisle towards Newcastle aboard one of the two-hourly stopping services and after 40 minutes – seven minutes beyond Haltwhistle – you will reach the first of four stations along this charming Tyne Valley route with mechanical signalling interest. Bardon Mill is a very quiet spot, as reflected in its 1874-vintage North Eastern Railway signal box, which has been routinely 'switched out' for as long as anyone can remember, certainly for at least the last 40 years!

Bardon Mill has been retained in order to break up the section from Haltwhistle to Haydon Bridge, but it is many years since it saw regular use. Meantime, the station platforms offer a view of the box, 200 yards west of the station, along with three of its four semaphore arms – an eastbound home signal beyond the box and, looking east, a starter in the Newcastle direction and an eastbound home signal, both of which are on brackets to the north side of the line.

Less than ten minutes after leaving Bardon Mill, the stopping service from Carlisle will pause again at another place with mechanical signalling, thankfully in daily use this time. Haydon Bridge is a delightfully quiet spot with an attractive 1877-vintage

Grand Central's 12.53 London King's Cross-Sunderland service passes Billingham's impressive signal box on 18 August 2017 and is about to pass a junction for the freight route to Seal Sands, which is controlled by signal B34.

Bardon Mill Signal Box on the Tyne Valley Line has been 'switched out' for as long as anyone can remember. On 19 June 2017, Northern Rail 156454 approaches with the 14.11 departure for Newcastle.

signal box controlling a level crossing at the west end of the station where there are also a pair of original North Eastern Railway trespass warning signs alongside the line.

This is also a great photo-spot, with all five of the semaphore arms in view from the platform ends – three in the westbound direction (no signal numbers are displayed) and two in the eastbound direction. There is also a footbridge around 400 yards west of the station with a good view back to the signal box. For a pleasant interlude between trains, I can recommend the Railway Hotel, just 200 yards from the station in the direction of the river (south).

Hexham is another well-preserved station and the most important calling point on the Tyne Valley Line. Its remarkable Grade II listed signal box stands on a gantry some 300 yards east of the station. This 1896-vintage North Eastern Railway box now only appears

to control two semaphore arms after the loss of its famously tall eastbound home HE3, now a colour light. The first of these is eastbound home HE10 at the end of platform 2 – where hourly terminating services return towards Newcastle and cross to the eastbound line just beyond the signal box. The other mechanical signal, which looks to be motor worked, is a westbound starter HE43, standing 400 yards beyond the station.

Last of the four locations with surviving semaphores along the Tyne Valley is probably the finest spot of all. While Prudhoe does not have any surviving station buildings, its tall signal box, alongside a level crossing to the west of the station, is one of the oldest and finest North Eastern Railway boxes to survive. It dates from the early 1870s and besides the level crossing controls seven semaphore arms, all but one of which are visible from the station.

Haydon Bridge must rank as one of the Tyne Valley Line's most photogenic locations, although its signal box name board is very faded. Here Northern Rail 156438 is about to pass non-stop on 19 June 2017 with the 11.35 Carlisle-Newcastle.

Hexham has only two surviving semaphore signals, but its Grade II listed signal box is an absolute gem. It is one of two similar surviving structures on the Tyne Valley Line, the other being at Wylam.

Super-power for a Tyne Valley freight service on 19 June 2017, where 66065/66+67007 approach Prudhoe with a service from Carlisle to Tyne Yard.

A trio of semaphore arms give the all clear to Scotrail 156430 as it approaches Prudhoe and its impressive signal box on 19 June 2017 with a Glasgow Central-Newcastle service.

In the eastbound (up) direction, these are outer home (PE15), home (PE16) starter (PE17) and advanced starter (PE18). In the westbound direction, a sighting board obscures home signal PE42, starter PE41 stands at the end of the down platform, while advanced starter PE40 also has a sighting board behind it and stands some 400 yards west of the station adjacent to a foot crossing of the line. This crossing offers a great vantage point from which to see the one signal PE15 not visible from the station and, looking back towards the box and station, all three other up signals. In contrast to the antiquity of the box, it is interesting to note that three of the signals (16, 40 and 42) are on what look like very modern galvanised steel posts.

Ashington-Newcastle

For a route that has seen only freight traffic since its closure to passengers in 1964, the line heading north-east from Newcastle to Bedlington and Ashington has done remarkably well to retain its traditional infrastructure. Much of the route is double track and there is a fine group of six North Eastern Railway signal boxes still in use and controlling a large array of semaphore signals, as well as level crossings at each of six locations.

My brief tour of this fascinating area in June 2017 was not well timed, as Lynemouth Power Station, which was previously the destination for a considerable volume of coal traffic, was undergoing conversion to biomass

England's most north-easterly manual signal box is at North Seaton, seen here on 20 June 2017 when services on the route to Lynemouth Power Station were suspended pending its conversion from coal to bio-mass firing.

firing. That meant that all traffic on the route north from Bedlington had been suspended until October 2017, although two signal boxes on the section of line north of West Sleekburn junction – at North Seaton and Marcheys House – remained staffed, despite the total lack of any train services!

North Seaton is one of the earliest surviving boxes in the UK, dating from 1872 and controlling a level crossing on the A196 at the site of the former North Seaton station, closed in November 1964. Approaching by road from the west, there is a splendid view of North Seaton Viaduct, a 14-span steel structure built in 1926 as replacement for an earlier wooden structure and known locally as the 'Black Bridge'. There are semaphore arms close to the box in both directions, and a good vantage point to see the box and up home, which is above a distant signal, is from a footbridge just north of the level crossing.

Heading south, the next box is Marcheys House, just to the south of North Seaton Viaduct and controlling the line northwards to North Seaton, southwards to Bedlington North and the north-to-east side of a triangular route to Cambois and North Blyth, where the eastern junction of this triangle is controlled by the nearby Winning Level Crossing box. Marcheys House box dates from 1895 and has a number of semaphores within easy view of the level crossing. Looking north there is a very modern looking pair of junction home and distant signals, while looking south where the line descends towards Bedlington, there are home and distant signals controlling both the main route and the line coming in from Winning.

A drive of less than a mile to the east and then south brings you to Winning, an identical North Eastern Railway design to Marcheys House, also dating from 1895. Here again, there are another pair of very modern looking home and distant signals (WG2 and WG3) standing close to the box and protecting the up line and junction towards Marcheys House. Looking west to the junction itself, there are home

signals, both obscured by sighting boards, protecting the two routes in the Blyth direction.

Little more than a mile south of Winning are the two signal boxes at either end of the former Bedlington Station, the single platform of which on the east side of the line and station building remain remarkably intact and awaiting the long-anticipated revival of passenger services between Newcastle and Ashington. Largest and most important of this pair is Bedlington North, which stands in the fork made by the line heading north to Ashington and Blyth and a connecting route heading north-west to Morpeth, where a triangular junction with the East Coast Main Line means it sees occasional use as a diversionary route.

Bedlington North box dates from 1912 and, besides a level crossing, has a number of semaphores under its control in the station area, as well as a number of colour lights on both the Morpeth branch and north towards the south end of the triangular junction, whose northern and eastern points are controlled by Marcheys House and Winning respectively. After my lack of luck in seeing any action further north, my patience at Bedlington was rewarded by the chance to photograph celebrity Class 66 locomotive 66779 *Evening Star* working a freight train from York to North Blyth.

To the south of the former station, and less than 300 yards from the north box, the smaller Bedlington South box controls a busy level crossing and signalling at the southern end of the station and southwards towards the final outpost of mechanical signalling on the route, at Newsham South. Unlike the north box, Bedlington South does not have any colour light signals under its control, while the signals controlled by both Bedlington boxes, like those at Winning, look remarkably recent installations.

Modern semaphore signals are also a feature at Newsham South, around two miles south of Bedlington and southern end of the double track route all the way

northward from here to Lynemouth and some way east of Winning on the Blyth line. Looking north from the level crossing here, there is an up home signal, with down starter signals protecting both lines some distance beyond, while looking south there is an up starter and then furthest away a down home signal. The box here once controlled a branch towards two former collieries, but now simply controls the route south to Benton Junction, at which point control of the line moves to the Tyneside regional signalling centre.

North Lincolnshire

Re-signalling in the Barnetby area at the end of 2015 may have removed some of the finest remaining semaphore signals on the national network, but it did not completely spell the end of mechanical signalling in North Lincolnshire. Limited

mechanical signalling remains on inaccessible and freight-only routes within Immingham Docks, but there are two other locations within this region that are well worth a visit, namely Gainsborough and at two locations on the branch line to Barton-on-Humber.

Gainsborough Central is one of three stations – along with Kirton Lindsey and Brigg – that see passenger trains only once a week, when on a Saturday there are three Sheffield-Cleethorpes services on this line, taking a far more direct route than the alternative via Lincoln. This 'Parliamentary' service is all that the line has enjoyed since weekday services were withdrawn in October 1993, although efforts are being made by local authorities and a rail promotion ground to reinstate regular weekday services.

While three other signal boxes along this 21-mile line – those at Northorpe, Kirton Lime Sidings and Brigg – only

Celebrity GBRf-owned 66779 *Evening Star* passes the closed Bedlington station on 20 June 2017 with a working from York to North Blyth, which is about to pass Bedlington North Signal Box.

have colour lights, Gainsborough Central not only retains semaphore signals, but three of its signals were actually renewed in 2017. These can all be seen from the station platforms, and comprise up home signal GC23, which stands just in front of the 1885-vintage signal box, along with down home GC2 and down starter GC3. Looking west there is also a tall up starter above a distant signal controlled by nearby Gainsborough Trent Junction Signal Box, whose only other remaining semaphore arm seems to be an up home signal controlling exit from the Brigg Line route.

Heading north-east from Gainsborough to the south bank of the Humber, the other fascinating outpost of mechanical signalling in the area is at New Holland and Goxhill on the ten-mile long Barton-on-Humber branch line. This route once served New Holland Pier, and provided a connection with Humber ferries to Hull, until opening of the Humber Bridge in June 1981 at which time a new curve opened at New Holland, and trains diverted westwards to Barton-on-Humber.

New Holland Pier remains an important freight loading point, although all traffic is now delivered by road, and a remaining spur off the branch has been blocked

close to Barrow Road Crossing. This is the first of three signal boxes and gated level crossings on the two-mile stretch of this line between New Holland and Goxhill, and close to the box stands an up home signal numbered OX28/BR5, to denote both the adjacent Barrow Road Crossing, as well as the nearby block post at Oxmarsh Crossing.

After passing Barrow Road's down home signal, the train pauses only moments later just beyond the Oxmarsh Crossing up home signal, where the single line token is surrendered to the signaller, who stands on a metal platform alongside the modern (1959) box. Passing another set of crossing gates, the train then crosses to the up line of what becomes a double-track alignment, and there is then a straight stretch of line to Goxhill.

At Goxhill an attractive Great Central Railway Box dating from 1910 stands south of the attractively preserved station building and a third set of wooden level crossing gates. Here there is an up home behind a sighting board at the north end of platform 1, with a down home signal just south of the box. An up outer home signal can also be seen in the distance, by looking back along the straight section of line towards New Holland.

Northern Rail 144010 approaches Gainsborough Central on 20 January 2018 with the Saturdays-only 13.03 to Cleethorpes, with signal box and new up home signal on the left.

CHAPTER 7

NORTH-WEST ENGLAND

J ust as it was the last outpost of steam on British Railways in 1968, so it is perhaps fitting that mechanical signalling has survived in more places across the North-West than in any other part of the United Kingdom, although the replacement process continues, and the Preston-Blackpool North branch will have lost its marvellous semaphores by the time these words are published.

Before looking at this line and other pockets of remaining semaphores, the right place to begin a tour of this region is on what must be the finest near-continuous stretch of mechanical signalling anywhere in Britain, the 94½-mile stretch of Cumbrian Coast extending from Arnside, north of Lancaster along what is called the Furness Line to Barrow-in-Furness, and then on up the Cumbrian Coast Line through Workington to Wigton, south-west of Carlisle.

This fascinating, and in parts highly scenic route, boasts no less than seventeen signal boxes and two gate boxes controlling semaphore signals, most of which are at, or close to, stations and so accessible to the rail-borne traveller. Getting around is relatively straightforward, with Northern Rail services along the routes being roughly hourly from Carlisle to Barrow, with a slightly higher frequency between Barrow and Lancaster, and the added bonus at the time of my April 2017 visit of two loco-hauled trains, with the published timetable even showing which services were scheduled for loco haulage. Adding further interest are the trains of nuclear flasks to and from the nuclear facilities along the route at Sellafield and Drigg.

Arnside

Leaving the West Coast Main Line at Carnforth, where on your left is the fine sight of a large collection of heritage locomotives and rolling stock owned and

Northern Rail 185134 departs Arnside on 6 April 2017 with the 13.38 to Barrow-in-Furness, passing its historic signal box and about to cross the 50-arch Arnside Viaduct.

operated by West Coast Railways, it is only a matter of ten minutes before you encounter semaphore signalling interest at the first of many photogenic places along the Furness Line. Arnside is a delightful spot with a Grade II listed Furness Railway signal box from 1897 standing just beyond the western end of the up platform and shortly before the line crosses the River Kent estuary on the 50-span Arnside Viaduct.

Three signals are visible from the platform, with an up starter at the eastern end of the station, a down home opposite the signal box and an up home at the end of the viaduct. Out of sight beyond are a down starter and an up distant, which is located at the far end of the viaduct. It is worth noting that most signals on the Furness and Cumbrian Coast routes are not plated with signal numbers, so numbers will only be mentioned at the few places where they are evident. Besides an excellent view of the signal box from the station footbridge, it is well worth taking a short walk to the waterfront, where there is a great view of the viaduct, with the semaphores either side of it, and there is also a very decent pub here, with a view out onto the viaduct.

Grange-over-Sands

Only five minutes after crossing the viaduct and then sweeping to the west, a long section of straight track close to the estuary shore brings you to the first mechanical signals at Grange-over-Sands, where a down home and up starter stand

DRS-owned 37401 *Mary Queen of Scots* approaches Grange-over-Sands on 6 April 2017 with Northern Rail's 10.53 departure for Barrow-in-Furness.

some 400 yards east of the delightful and Grade II listed station. The line then curves to the right before passing the 1956 British Rail London Midland region box, which stands just west of the station on the seaward side, between the railway and the Cumbrian Coastal Way footpath.

An up home stands opposite the box, while beyond there is a down starter some distance further on, but easily seen and photographed from a public park running alongside the railway. This is a delightful spot to view trains and signals, with the first of two fine vantage points being a footbridge east of the station and easily reached along the coastal path. For a good view of the down starter and the up outer home beyond it, go into the park on the town side of the railway and stand close to, or on, the fifth bench along, where a helpfully low fence gives a fine view of the two signals as the line curves round to the left.

Ulverston

This charming town, and the birthplace of comedian Stan Laurel of Laurel and Hardy fame, boasts another attractive Grade II listed station, which opened in 1874, replacing an earlier Furness Railway terminus station on completion of the route to Barrow. It has an unusual layout similar to that at Yeovil Pen Mill in having an island platform and a main down platform with platform 2 not in regular use (and not numbered) so all up trains serve platform 3 and down train doors are only opened on platform 1.

Loco-haulage by DRS-owned Class 37s was an attractive feature of Cumbrian Coast services. Here, 37405 has just left Ulverston on 5 April 2017 with Northern Rail's 11.12 to Barrow-in-Furness.

Signalling interest here comprises an up starter just beyond the platform ends, with a down home alongside the far disused end of the island platform. The signal box stands some 400 yards west of the station, with a down starter beyond, immediately in front of a bridge carrying the A590 trunk road and a home signal in the up direction, with shunting arm for access to a siding almost opposite the signal box. Besides shots on the station itself, the best vantage point for photos requires a 15-minute walk from the station to the A590 over-bridge, where a thankfully low parapet gives an uninterrupted view towards the signal box and station.

Dalton/Park South

Roughly mid-way between Ulverston and Barrow trains call at Dalton, beyond which, and after passing through the

223-yard long Dalton Tunnel, the line reaches Dalton Junction, where a 1902 Furness Railway box controls a junction between the loop into Barrow and a short cut-off route between here and nearby Park South. Mechanical signalling, however, is limited at both boxes, with Dalton Junction having no semaphores on the main line, but controlling a down section signal on the cut-off line, which is just visible from a passing train, with a distant below that is controlled by Park South box. Park South has two further semaphores, both in the down direction. These are a home signal standing 400 yards before the box and controlling exit from cut-off line and a single semaphore beyond the junction north of the box and level crossing.

Barrow

Barrow-in-Furness is one of the least attractive places on the Cumbrian Coast

Barrow-in-Furness is an interesting location, with a fine array of semaphores controlled by a 1907 Furness Railway signal box. On 5 April 2017, 37401 heads onto the single track section to Park Junction with the 17.31 to Carlisle.

route, but the busy modern station, a 1950s replacement for a station that was destroyed by a German bomb in 1941, is well worth a visit for its signalling interest. A 1907 Furness Railway box stands at the western end of the three-platform complex, close to the sizeable diesel stabling point, which is full of stock on a Sunday, but completely empty during weekdays.

Approaching from the Lancaster direction, the only semaphore you pass is a tall up advanced starter, a few hundred yards before the station itself. Here, there are up starters for the two through platforms (1 & 2) while at the western end there are down home signals for these two – rare examples installed in 1940, according to a local railwayman I spoke to – both with shunting arms for access to the diesel depot, and another for platform 3, a dead-end used by terminating services from Carlisle.

Beyond the signal box a starter controls exit from a loop onto the single track section to Park South Junction, while in the up direction a junction signal has two main arms with shunting arms below. For a great shot of departing services towards Carlisle – including the Class 37s at the head of loco-hauled services, which were always at the Carlisle end of their trains – take a ten-minute walk along Holker Street to the football ground, where there is a junction with Devonshire Road and an excellent vantage point for photos (except on sunny mornings).

Beginning an early morning foray from Barrow felt like a throwback to the 1980s and a departure for the West Highland Line from Glasgow Queen Street as 37401 *Mary Queen of Scots* – in BR large logo blue livery and complete with Highland Terrier logo – eased its four-coach train past Barrow signal box before opening up the distinctive English Electric engines on the 05.49 departure for Sellafield and Carlisle. There were already a fair scattering of Sellafield workers on board for their 70-minute

commute to the nuclear plant, with many more joining at the stations and request stops en route. Operation of the two loco-hauled sets (which ended in December 2018) was geared around the needs of Sellafield staff, with this service arriving at 06.56, while the second set, powered by 37409 *Lord Hinton* on the day of my April 2017 trip, arrives in Sellafield from Carlisle at 06.52.

Askam

Shortly after passing Park South Junction where, as mentioned above, the only semaphore in evidence on the main route stands north of the level crossing, and just 10 minutes from the industrial town of Barrow comes a marked contrast in the small town of Askam. Here, the remarkable chalet-style station building stands alongside an equally attractive Furness Railway signal box, dating from 1895. Four semaphore arms are visible from the platforms, with a down home 100 yards south of the signal box and level crossing and an up starter at the platform end. North of the station there is an up home signal, with a down starter some distance further out.

DRS-owned 37604/059 approach Askam on 4 April 2017 with a British Nuclear Fuels train conveying nuclear flasks from Sellafield to Crewe.

Unlike other nuclear workings, traffic from Sellafield to Heysham is usually worked in top-and-tail mode to eliminate the need for a run round at its final destination. On 5 April 2017, 37609/218 approach Foxfield, bound for Heysham Harbour Power Station.

Foxfield

This is a really delightful and isolated spot, and the first of three request stops with signal boxes on the section of line between Barrow and Workington. The 1879 Furness Railway wooden signal box stands at the north end of an island platform, with five semaphore arms in view – two to the south and three to the north. Sadly out of view are distant signals – the down example can be reached by road, but the up distant is on the opposite side of a viaduct across the nearby estuary, so pretty inaccessible, though just visible from the station platform. There is an excellent panoramic view of the line looking north from the station entrance as it sweeps away to the left past an up home and round to an advanced starter on the down line.

Millom

A small 1891 Furness Railway box at Millom stands beyond a road over-bridge to the north of the station platforms, from where four semaphore arms can be seen. To the south, where the line curves to the left, is an up starter, while in the down direction there is a home signal at the platform end and a starter some distance away. An up home signal stands close to the signal box, where there is also a trailing crossover and a short siding on the downside. On the up platform, the former station building is now occupied by the Millom Heritage Museum, which also operates one of the handful of independently-run ticket offices on the rail network (other examples being Ledbury and Pembrey & Burry Port), although run to help fund the museum rather than as a commercial venture.

Silecroft

North of Millom the train passes two gate boxes at Kirksanton and Limestone Hall, the latter being only just south of the next signal box on the route at Silecroft, another

Mixed rolling stock at Millom on 4 April 2017, where the 14.50 to Lancaster comprises Pacer unit 142031 sandwiched between single cars 153307 and 153301.

of the line's many request stops. Here, the Furness Railway box from 1923 stands south of the down (northbound) platform, controlling level crossing barriers and a small number of mechanical signals. These are a down distant close to Limestone Hall crossing, a home signal close to the station and a starter 400 yards to the north. There are no semaphores in the up direction but the box does also control a crossover immediately south of the station and with mechanical points and disc signals.

Bootle

Bootle is another delightfully quiet spot, and third of three request stops with signalling interest, where the diminutive signal box, reputedly dating from 1871, stands at the north end of the down platform and next to a pair of metal

A pair of single car units (153378/330) passes the Furness Railway signal box at Silecroft on 4 April 2017 and is about to call with the 13.08 service to Carlisle.

One of Britain's oldest surviving signal boxes is this Furness Railway design from 1871 at Bootle. Northern Rail 156469 arrives at the station on 4 April 2017 with the 12.40 departure for Lancaster.

crossing gates. Besides these, it controls an up starter some 400 yards south of the station, where a white sighting background has been cleverly painted on a bridge immediately behind the signal, a down home in front of the box and looking further north a down starter, with large sighting board behind, and an up home signal. There is a splendid vantage point to photograph northbound trains – and particularly the Class 37s – from a spot in a nearby coal yard (accessed by permission) about 200 yards north of the level crossing.

Sellafield

This is a fascinating location, but difficult to photograph, not least due to the fence along the down platform (2) which is actually an island platform with a disused face onto the up platform. The signal box stands at the north end of platform 2 and has a metal platform alongside for token exchange. Another impressive feature here is a pair of water columns at each end of the station with a brick water tower standing some distance north of the station. There are a number of signals south of the station controlling access to the nuclear complex, with a pair of down home signals allowing trains to use either platform and an up home at the end of platform 1. There are down starters and shunting discs controlling the north end of the station and access to a siding at the start of the single track, while in the up (southbound) direction there are home and outer home signals visible from the station.

Token exchange at Sellafield on 4 April 2017, where the driver of 153378/330 has just handed over the token for the single line section from St. Bees and is about to call at the station with the 11.08 departure for Barrow-in-Furness.

St. Bees

St Bees is an attractive spot and the only passing loop on the single line from Sellafield to Whitehaven. Its charming and unique chalet-style signal box stands to the west of the line at the north end of the down platform. It controls level crossing barriers and has five semaphores – in the down (northbound) direction there is a home at the southern end of the passing loop, a starter alongside the box and an advanced starter a short distance beyond at the end of the loop. In the up direction there is a home signal beyond points for the loop and a starter at the end of the up platform, where a disc signal also controls access to a short siding.

St. Bees is another photogenic location on the Cumbrian Coast. Here 156484 has just left the station on 3 April 2017 with the 14.40 to Carlisle and is about to exit the station passing loop.

Whitehaven

Towards the end of the lengthy single line section from Sellafield, the train pauses at another request stop called Corkickle, where there is a semaphore acting as a down starter, before the train enters the 1,322-yard long Whitehaven Tunnel. Whitehaven station itself, at the northern end of this tunnel, is not an easy location to photograph, with only a single through platform and Bransty signal box standing north of the station at the point where the double track resumes, but obscured from view by a rather unsightly Network Rail portacabin-type structure. The up starter (BY4) is a colour light but at the north end there are semaphore home signals for both the through platform (2) and the bay platform (1) which is used by terminating services from Carlisle. The only other arm in view is an a starter some distance north of the signal box.

Workington

Workington is one of the few places left, along with Bedlington, Worcester and Shrewsbury, able to boast of having more than one mechanical signal box, although the number of remaining mechanical signals here seems rather low. To the south of the spacious station a home and distant stand close to Workington Main No. 2 signal box control southbound exit

Workington is a shadow of its former self, but still has signal boxes at each end of the station. On 3 April 2017, 37401 *Mary Queen of Scots* passes Workington Main No. 2 box at the south end as it approaches the station with the 13.32 to Carlisle.

37401 *Mary Queen of Scots* retains its Highland Terrier logo and historic BR 'large logo' livery. Here it is about to leave Workington on 3 April 2017 with the 13.32 to Carlisle.

from the goods loop, so presumably see relatively little use, with the up home on platform 1 being a light.

To the north of the station, Workington Main No. 3 box stands at the end of the up platform, with a down starter and another close to it controlling exit from the western freight loop. North of the station, and visible from a footbridge and a footpath running between the railway and the rugby league ground, are a down advanced starter and an up home, with a distant below and a shunting arm to its right. Unlike the other semaphore here, this is plated (WN3+WN41/42).

Wigton

Maryport can boast another impressive signal box, but the only remaining mechanical signalling is a few shunting discs to the south of the station. There is one final outpost of mechanical signalling

Most modern of all the Cumbrian Coast's fine collection of signal boxes is this 1957 BR design at Wigton, seen here on 3 April 2017 as 37401 powers away from the station with the 09.01 to Barrow-in-Furness.

on the Cumbrian Coast route, however, at Wigton, birthplace of broadcaster Melvyn Bragg and a rather basic station now, with nicely kept gardens tended by local volunteers on the down platform.

There are only colour lights north of the station, but looking south from the fine, but rusty, station footbridge, up home WN37 stands just beyond the end of the southbound platform with the modern (1957) signal box on the west side of the line 300 yards beyond and a down home signal still further down the line. A siding on the east serves a large industrial complex but does not appear to see any regular traffic.

SETTLE & CARLISLE LINE

Having reached Carlisle on the Cumbrian Coast Line, it is time to make a return south along England's most scenic railway line, the Settle & Carlisle route, famously reprieved from closure in 1989 and now a hugely popular attraction for tourists and leisure travellers that is actively promoted by a voluntary support group, the Friends

of the Settle-Carlisle Line, whose members also provide guides on certain trains, a refreshment trolley service between Settle and Appleby and buffet services at a number of stations.

For those with an interest in mechanical signalling, there is still plenty to appreciate along the route, with nine signal boxes between Carlisle and Hellifield, to the south of Settle, retaining at least some semaphore signalling. The rail-borne traveller will only be able to catch brief glimpses of the first three boxes south of Carlisle – Howe & Co's Siding, Low House Crossing and Culgaith, with the first opportunity to appreciate the route's mechanical signalling coming at its most important intermediate station.

Appleby

Appleby North is a relatively modern box, opened in 1951 to replace an earlier structure that had been destroyed by fire. It stands a short distance to the north of the station platforms on the east side of

Historic lamp standards on the platform give a truly authentic feel to Appleby station, with its restored Midland Railway station buildings and working water tower. On 2 August 2017, Northern Rail 158817 departs with the 11.36 to Carlisle.

the line, controlling the station area and sidings that also form a physical link with the partly-preserved Eden Valley Darlington to Penrith route (closed in 1962) that served nearby Appleby East station. This route is being slowly restored by the Eden Valley Railway Trust, with the hope of eventually reaching the former Kirkby Stephen East station, 11 miles to the south and subject of a separate restoration project by the Stainmore Railway Company.

Semaphore signalling at Appleby comprises a total of six arms on the main line, with a shunt signal mounted alongside the down home signal for access to sidings near the box and the former link to the Eden Valley route. Looking north from the station, the furthest signals are a down starter and an outer home in the up direction. Close to the box, the up home is mounted on a modern looking bracket immediately adjacent to the signal box. To the south of the station, an up starter stands 200 yards

south of the platform end – which features a working water column used for steam specials – with a down outer home signal just beyond.

Kirkby Stephen

Heading south on one of the most scenic stretches of the line, the next box after Appleby North is at Kirkby Stephen, or Kirkby Stephen West, as it was once known. Like Appleby, Kirkby Stephen is another of the fine Midland Railway stations that has been superbly restored thanks to the efforts of the Settle & Carlisle Railway Trust, with waiting rooms on both platforms, traditional lamp standards, and the main station building now used as holiday accommodation.

The modern BR (LMR) 1974-vintage box stands just south of the station where there are sidings on both sides of the line and an old goods shed beyond. Only two

Making a stark contrast to another extremely well-preserved Midland Railway station is this British Railways designed box dating from 1974 at Kirkby Stephen. On 31 July 2017, Northern Rail 158843 is about to call at the station with the 14.32 to Carlisle.

of the four remaining semaphores can be seen from the platform, with a down (northbound) home signal opposite the box and a down starter some distance beyond the platform end. In the up direction, a home signal stands behind a brick bridge carrying a farm track just north of the station, while the up starter is some way south, round a curve beyond the old goods shed. This is another photogenic spot, with a good vantage point from the station footbridge.

Garsdale

Less than 15 minutes south from Kirkby Stephen, and after travelling over Ais Gill Summit, the train reaches another signalled location at remote Garsdale. This isolated spot was once a junction for the 40-mile long Wensleydale railway to Hawes and Northallerton, and boasts another superbly restored (Grade II listed) station, complete with 1910 Midland Railway signal box on the down platform, also Grade II listed.

Garsdale was once known as Hawes Junction, and earned its place in Britain's signalling history following the Hawes Junction accident on Christmas Eve 1910, when a northbound express train ploughed into the back of two light engines just north of the station. The accident was caused because the signalman had forgotten about the light engines before clearing the line for the express at a time when track circuiting,

Network Rail's 'flying banana' – the New Measurement Train (NMT) – passes the historic station at Garsdale on 31 July 2017 while working from Heaton (Newcastle) to York.

which would have prevented such a tragedy, had not been fully adopted by the Midland Railway. Following a Board of Trade report into the accident, track circuiting was installed here and right across the company's network.

As at Kirkby Stephen, the box here once again has four semaphores under its control. Looking north from the up station platform (on which I had the precious sighting of a red squirrel!) you will see the down starter and further out the up home, with the down advanced starter just visible as the line sweeps around to the left beyond the former Junction. Looking south, again around a left hand bend, the up starter can just be seen some 300 yards away. Don't miss on this platform the statue of Ruswarp, the dog which famously played a part in saving the route from closure in the late 1980s.

Blea Moor

Continuing our journey south, the Leeds-bound train will take just five minutes to reach its next calling point, Dent, which at 1,150 feet has the distinction of being England's highest main line station, though sadly its signal box, like so many others along the line, has long since closed (January 1981, then destroyed by fire in September 1984). From Dent, the train then passes through the longest of the route's 14 tunnels, the 1½ mile (2,629 yard-long) Blea Moor Tunnel, before emerging in a cutting then sweeping round a left hand bend passing Blea Moor Signal Box and onto the famous Ribblehead Viaduct.

Having previously visited Scotland's remotest signal box (Glenwhilly) it seemed only right to make the effort to get to England's remotest box. Blea Moor stands about a mile north of Ribblehead station and is separated from it by the 440 yard long, 24 arch Viaduct. Getting to the box is a fairly challenging 30 minute walk from Ribblehead station, taking a path which heads under the Viaduct before bearing off to the right onto a path signed 'Whernside

4½'. For the best vantage point, continue past the box and make for a bridge carrying a farm track, which stands some distance beyond (good walking shoes or boots essential).

For all the panoramic view towards the box and viaduct in one direction and Blea Moor Tunnel in the opposite direction, there is little remaining mechanical signalling interest at Blea Moor, where most of the key signals are modern single aspect lights. There are just four remaining semaphores, all being in the up direction, with just one of these – an up home signal immediately north of the bridge – seeing regular use. Alongside it is a small shunting arm to access the up goods loop, while the other two semaphores are one controlling exit from this loop and one to the right of the down line, which is presumably used to signal the daily evening service that terminates at Ribblehead and would reverse here before returning south.

Settle Junction

Carrying on south from Ribblehead, the train will pause at Horton-in-Ribblesdale then pass a rail-served quarry on the west side of the line that seems to generate significant freight on to the line. Next up is Settle, another charmingly restored station in a delightful market town, where the signalling interest lies in the preserved Settle station signal box, closed in 1984, but preserved and re-sited to a position north of the up platform in 1997, with a couple of preserved semaphore signals nearby. It is open to visitors on Saturdays during the summer.

Two miles south of Settle stands a remarkably similar looking box at Settle Junction, where the main route from Carlisle is joined from the right by the double track Bentham Line to Carnforth and Lancaster. Like Blea Moor, Settle Junction, a 1913 Midland Railway box, takes a bit of reaching, being alongside the narrow and busy A65 trunk Road, with no

DRS-owned 66303 approaches Settle Junction on 1 August 2017 with a very short freight train from Carlisle to Crewe. The route to the left is the Bentham Line to Carnforth and Morecambe.

footpath. In the interests of safety, I opted for a taxi, which was able to drop me opposite the box.

From here, a perilous walk some 300 yards back towards Settle along the A65 takes you to a farm track over-bridge which gives you a marvellous vantage point in both directions. Looking north towards Settle where the two routes divide some 300 yards beyond the bridge, there are down starting and up outer home signals on each route. Turning back towards the box and junction there are up home signals protecting each route, while some way beyond the box stands a two-arm bracket, with the S&C- bound arm at a higher level, to denote the principal route.

Hellifield

Last, but by no means least, of the Settle & Carlisle Line's mechanical signalling delights is Hellifield, a magnificently restored Grade II listed building on

an island platform, with an array of semaphores to savour at both ends of the platform. The star turn here is the rare shunting signal on a square wooden post controlling exit from a down goods loop at the north end of the station. The post has apparently been restored in the past, but now looks in need of some TLC and stands alongside a much more modern tubular post, so its survival is something of a miracle.

Beyond these two at the north end of the station is a down starter on a bracket with another shunting arm. Looking south, Hellifield South Junction signal box, a Midland Railway design from 1911, stands at the far end of the platform, where the Clitheroe line branches off to the right from the main line to Skipton and Leeds. An up home on platform one stands a short distance in front of a bracket, which has separate arms for each route, while in the down direction there are home signals on both the main line and on the Clitheroe route, each with shunting arms to the left.

Blackpool North branch

Blackpool was one of the last outposts of steam working in Britain – only succumbing with the very end of steam working in August 1968, so it is appropriate that Blackpool North could boast the finest collection of mechanical signals at any seaside terminus for almost half a century more, until their oft-delayed replacement as part of a major upgrading and electrification of the 17½ mile long branch from Preston on the West Coast Main Line, which was finally undertaken in late 2017.

While the eastern end of this route had signal boxes at Kirkham and Salwick, there was no remaining mechanical interest at either location. This was confined to the 3¼ mile section from Blackpool North to Poulton-le-Fylde, which boasted three

remaining boxes – Blackpool North No.2, Carleton Crossing and Poulton-le-Fylde No. 3, one-time junction for a branch to Fleetwood. Another longstanding survivor on this section of line, Blackpool North No. 1, had been abolished in January 2011.

At the eight-platform terminus, Blackpool North No. 2 box stood on the north side of the lines into the station, controlling a fine array of semaphore arms, with individual arms controlling exit from platforms 1 and 2 and pairs of semaphores for platforms 3&4, 5&6 and 7&8. There were then three home and distant starters, with shunting arms beneath each, at the station's throat, and in front of the signal box. The box itself, which was looking pretty much in need of a lick of paint at the time of my June 2016 visit, was a Lancashire & Yorkshire Railway design dating back

The wooden post of this notable shunting signal at Hellifield has been the subject of some discreet repair, so is not wholly original. On 1 August 2017, Northern Rail 142071 has just left the historic station with the 09.10 departure for Morecambe.

A farewell look at the old Blackpool North before its closure in November 2017 for re-building and electrification. On 22 September 2017, Northern Rail 156491/428 pass its fine collection of semaphore signals with the 10.40 departure for Manchester Airport.

to 1896, but another historic structure whose architectural integrity had been compromised by the installing of modern uPVC windows.

Returning to pay my last respects in late September 2017, I found a great deal had changed. The station layout had been severely rationalised earlier in the year, with platforms 1&2 and 7&8 having been razed to the ground as part of the upgrade programme, leaving just the middle two island platforms (3&4 + 5&6) in use until final closure of the existing station on Saturday, 11 November 2017. Being on an officially-organised visit by Network Rail this time, I was able to see that Blackpool North No. 2 Box now had only 28 remaining operational signal levers on its 90 lever frame.

Having left Blackpool North, the next sighting of mechanical signalling was at the line's first intermediate station, Layton, where a distant signal at the eastern end of the up platform was one of four semaphore arms controlled by

Carleton Crossing box, a short distance beyond Layton station. This small and attractive 12-lever box was a London & North Western Railway design, built after grouping of the railways by the London Midland & Scottish Railway in 1924, and controlled home and distant signals in each direction, with the down distant being below Poulton-le-Fylde's section signal.

Finally, the most important intermediate stop on this branch is the charmingly preserved Poulton-le-Fylde station, with its large island platform and junction with the 'mothballed' (now officially decommissioned by Network Rail) route to Fleetwood. Here the 1896-vintage Lancashire & Yorkshire Railway signal box stood in the fork between the two routes just west of the station. Semaphores visible from the station platform were an up starter (PT69) with sighting board behind, just in front of a road bridge east of the station, and junction arms (not plated with numbers)

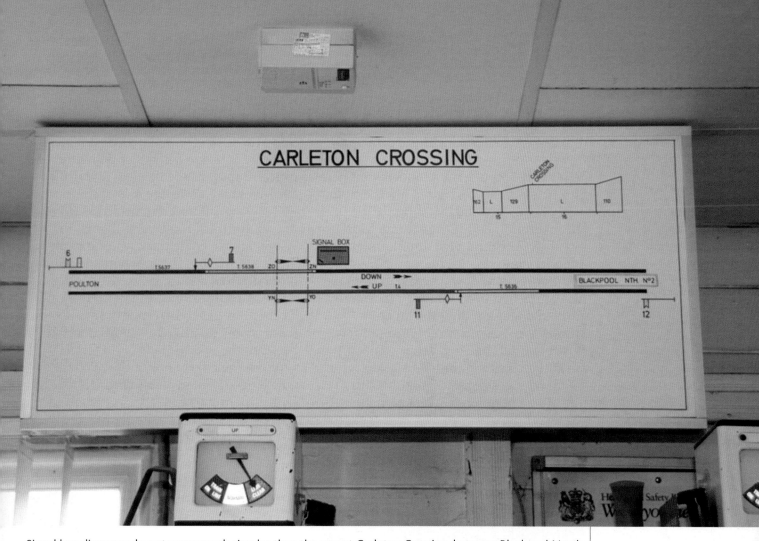

Signal box diagrams do not come much simpler than the one at Carleton Crossing, between Blackpool North and Poulton-le-Fylde, showing just home and distant signals in each direction. Up distant signal (12) stood on the platform at nearby Layton station.

Poulton-le-Fylde is a beautifully preserved station and former junction for the route to Fleetwood, a potential re-opening candidate. On 15 June 2016, Northern Rail 150119 departs for Blackpool North, with Poulton No. 3 Signal Box just visible beyond the bridge.

in the down direction at the platform end, with a taller left hand arm denoting that the line to Blackpool was the principal route.

As at Blackpool, my farewell visit here in September 2017 showed a fair amount had already changed in anticipation of electrification and re-signalling. Most notably, the brand new double-track junction onto the Fleetwood line – which reputedly never saw a single train make use of it – had been removed in March 2017 and along with it the junction arm at the western end of the station. Visiting Poulton No. 3 box revealed a similar picture of rationalisation to that at the seaside terminus, with just nine operational levers along its 74-lever frame.

Rainford Junction marks the end of double track from the Wigan Wallgate direction and the start of token-controlled single line working to Kirkby. On 10 June 2017, the driver of 142007 has just collected the token and departs with the 12.10 to Kirkby.

Rainford Junction

Mid-way between Liverpool and Wigan, Rainford Junction is a rather delightful and peaceful spot, where the heavily fortified 1874-vintage Lancashire & Yorkshire Railway signal box controls access from the double track route running east to Wigan onto a single track leading to the buffers at Kirkby. This is where the hourly Northern Rail service from Manchester and Blackburn connects with Merseyrail electric services to Liverpool, although there is now no physical connection between the two sections of line.

No evidence remains of the two lines which once diverged at Rainford – to Ormskirk in the north and St. Helens to the south – so the box simply handles

and exchanges single line tokens with the hourly passenger services and the occasional freight services from Knowsley Freight Terminal, which is close the Kirkby on the south side of the line. There are four semaphore signals here, home and starter in each direction, with the down starter being on a bracket just beyond the box. All are easily photographed from the platforms and footbridge, with a pleasant pub, appropriately called The Junction, close by.

Parbold and Chapel Lane Crossing

Just ten miles north of Rainford and on a different route – the branch from Wigan to Southport – is another outpost of mechanical signalling in this area. These are the boxes at Parbold and at nearby Chapel Lane Crossing. Parbold is a really delightful spot, just over ten minutes on a Southport-bound train from Wigan Wallgate, which is located alongside the town's main station, Wigan North Western, on the WCML. Here, a listed 1877 Lancashire & Yorkshire Railway box, called Parbold Cabin, stands at the eastern end of the station, controls level crossing barriers and a trio of semaphore arms.

In the down (Southport) direction, there are a home signal (PB19) and starter (PB18) while in the up direction home signal PB4 on the up platform is a light, but starter PB5 is a semaphore that is mounted above a distant controlled by Chapel Lane Crossing. This crossing

The listed Parbold Cabin Signal Box can be seen in the background as Northern Rail 156427/142052 approach its up starter – with Chapel Lane Crossing's distant beneath – while forming the 16.40 departure for Manchester Airport on 21 September 2017.

Northern Rail 150111 approaches Chapel Lane Crossing on 21 September 2017 with the 15.03 Manchester Airport-Southport. The distant signal here is controlled by nearby Parbold Cabin.

can be reached by taking a pleasant 15 minute walk along the Leeds and Liverpool Canal from close to Parbold station. The box is little more than a Portacabin controlling gates on a farm track, that remain closed to road vehicles unless a button is pressed to request they are opened, but this is another spot with photographic potential.

Here, in the down direction, is the Parbold distant below a home signal protecting the crossing, with another single home arm in the up direction. That gives Chapel Lane Crossing three semaphores, the same as Parbold, although the two home signals protecting the crossing remain in the off position unless a vehicle has requested to cross the line. Midway between the two boxes there is another fine vantage point from a bridge carrying the A5209, where there is a good view of Chapel Lane Crossing and its signals looking eastwards, while from the pavement side of the bridge, Parbold

Cabin can be seen as the line sweeps round a left hand bend, with a good view of up trains passing PB5.

Midge Hall

One final location in this part of West Lancashire where mechanical signalling remains, and which can be seen from a passing train is Midge Hall, a long-closed station a few miles south-west of Preston on the route to Ormskirk where, as at Kirkby, there is a same platform connection with a Merseyrail service to Liverpool, but no remaining physical connection between the two sections of line. The 1972 BR LMR Type 15 Box at Midge Hall controls a level crossing and the token section south to the line's only passing loop at Rufford station, and has just one remaining semaphore, a home signal in the down (northbound) direction.

Helsby Junction and Ellesmere Port

Head south-west on a service from Warrington towards Chester and the first sight of mechanical signalling you once got is the signal box standing at the rather remote Frodsham Junction, on a tall embankment around a mile east of Frodsham station, where there is a semaphore to be seen on the recently-revived Halton Curve and others controlling the Junction onto it. Sadly, its semaphores have now been replaced, as part of the Halton Curve revival, but five minutes after pausing at Frodsham's award winning station, the next stop you reach is a veritable Mecca for mechanical signalling, Helsby.

Here, both station buildings and Helsby Junction Signal Box are Grade II listed, with the box standing at the north end of platforms 2 and 3 in the fork made by the route to Chester and the Cinderella line to Ellesmere Port, which is served by platforms 3 and 4. I counted nine semaphore arms visible from the platform, the star of which is the co-acting pair at the north end of platform 4. Having already seen and photographed the only two other examples left on the national network (Cantley and Greenloaning) it was something of a thrill when the pair were pulled off to allow the 16.14 from Ellesmere Port to Warrington Bank Quay to pass, pretty much the only time these signals could regularly be seen in the off position in the 2017 timetable.

Planned replacement of the signals at Cantley and Greenloaning means the last co-acting signal on the national network is likely to be this one at Helsby, seen here on 10 June 2017 as Northern Rail 150138 departs with the 16.14 to Warrington.

Ellesmere Port once generated a huge volume of freight traffic, controlled by a number of signal boxes. Today, the last survivor is 1972-vintage Ellesmere Port No. 4, seen in the distance on 10 June 2017 as 150138 departs with the 15.34 to Helsby.

In addition to this pair (HY38), the other signals at the north end of the station are down starter HY37 and advanced starter HY36 visible through a road over-bridge. Looking south towards Chester, up starter HY3 stands at the end of platform one, with a down home signal (HY42) around 100 yards beyond, and an advanced up starter (HY4) and down outer home (HY43) visible some distance away. Looking towards the Ellesmere Port line there are starters from both platform 3 (HY7) and platform 4 (HY11).

Besides the many opportunities on the station itself, there is a good vantage point from the over-bridge carrying Lower Rake Lane, just a three minute walk from the station. Here you will see a pair of up home signals that are not visible from the platform and get a good view of northbound services passing the down advanced starter as the line sweeps round a right hand curve.

Reaching Ellesmere Port from Helsby gives you a chance to ride on one of the country's least used sections of line – the 2017 timetable showed four trains a day on Monday to Saturday, and I was one of only two passengers on the 15.17 from Helsby when I travelled the line on a Saturday in June 2017. At Ellesmere Port station, trains from Helsby use platform 2, while platform 1 is served by Merseyrail electrics from Hooton.

Little remains of the once vast array of sidings and the last signal box to survive here is Ellesmere Port No. 4, a BR London Midland Region box from 1972 built on the base of a much earlier LNWR building destroyed by fire, which stands some 400 yards east of the station. It controls a number of semaphore arms at the Helsby end of the station, as well as two-aspect colour lights at the Hooton end of the station. Trains returning to Helsby from platform 2 join the down line at a crossover close to the box.

Manchester–Buxton

Taking a chance to visit surviving semaphore outposts in the Buxton area, I was keen to visit the two boxes on the freight-only Midland Railway route as well as the three remaining boxes on the Buxton line that are located at stations. Having carefully studied maps of the area, I alighted at Dove Holes, penultimate stop on the Buxton Line, from where a pleasant 1½ mile walk south from the station, across the A6 and along Dale Road, got me to the first and most impressive location, Peak Forest South.

The station here closed in 1967, but the station building remains as offices for DB Schenker and from an overbridge on Batham Gate Road, there is a splendid view looking south towards the signal box, signals and a handful of Class 66 and 60 locos awaiting their next duties. Sadly, on a Saturday afternoon there was no action to savour, when even the promised light engine movements failed to materialise.

Heading away from the line in the Buxton direction takes you to a turn called School Road in the village of Peak Dale. Head down here for about a mile and a left turn onto Waterswallows Road brings you to the second semaphore location at Tarmac's Tunstead Quarry. From another road over-bridge, the second box, Great Rocks Junction, is visible immediately in front of you, with sidings and access

A quiet Saturday afternoon scene at Peak Forest South on 3 June 2017, where a trio of Class 60/66 locos wait for their next aggregates duties alongside the 1925 Midland Railway signal box.

On the train, the destination display reads:

1st 14:29 Manchester Pic | On

2nd Terminates here
14:19:44

Way[...]

🚕 Taxi rank →

🚌 Buses ↘

Buxton's attractive 1894 signal box stands some distance north of the terminus station. On 3 June 2017, Northern Rail 150210/201 are signalled to depart with the 14.29 to Manchester Piccadilly.

to Tunstead Quarry, and the end of the double track route from the north.

Turning in a westerly direction away from Great Rocks, a slightly arduous three mile walk along Waterswallows Road (no pavement!) brings you into Buxton, where the attractive 1894 LNWR signal box stands 300 yards north of the station and controls access to the station as well as the freight routes south to Briggs Sidings and the eastward loop to Great Rocks Junction. It is possible to get a closer view of the box from between the three rail bridges spanning Lightwood Road, but there does not seem to be any better vantage point than the north end of platform 2 at Buxton station.

Departing from Buxton by train gives a good view of the box and the semaphores it controls on the station approach and the two freight branches. Then, just ten minutes later come the first of three locations with semaphores on the route north towards Manchester. This is Chapel-en-le-Frith, a delightful station standing above and some distance from the town it

serves and one with a sad place in railway history.

Here, a London & North Western Railway signal box was destroyed by a freight train suffering a brake failure on 9 February 1957, in an accident which killed the driver of 8F locomotive 48188, John Axon, who was posthumously awarded the George Cross for his bravery. A new BR London Midland Region type 15 box was opened in March 1957 as its replacement and remains in use today, although 'switched out' on the Saturday afternoon of my visit in June 2017.

Another ten minutes on from the splendid isolation of Chapel-en-le-Frith comes the next semaphore outpost on the Buxton route at Furness Vale, a rather pleasant spot where a London & North Western box dating from 1887 controls a level crossing immediately north of the station platforms and has a total of six semaphores – home and starter signals can be seen in each direction and the station footbridge making a good vantage point.

Chapel-en-le-Frith is an attractive rural location and scene of a famous railway accident in February 1957, which cost the lives of two railwaymen and saw destruction of its original signal box. On 3 June 2017, Northern Rail 150118/117 approach the replacement box with the 14.29 to Manchester Piccadilly.

Sadly, neither of its working distant signals are in view from the station area. For an interlude between trains, a pub called The Crossings alongside the down platform makes a pleasant port of call and has a number of items of railway memorabilia displayed in the bar.

One final area of semaphore interest on this route, though not readily accessible to the rail-borne passenger, is Norbury Crossing, a small gate-box on the north side of the line between Middlewood and Hazel Grove stations. In the Manchester-bound direction, the most accessible of its signals is a distant signal located at the southern end of Middlewood station, with its down home signal some way between the station and crossing. From a passing train I was not able to see any other semaphores, but noted that its up home signal, just north of the crossing, is a colour light.

Furness Vale is another charming location, with an LNWR signal box dating from 1887. Here, Northern Rail 150201/210 are about to call with the 16.26 departure for Buxton.

Manchester–Sheffield via the Hope Valley

Take the Hope Valley stopping service from Manchester Piccadilly to Sheffield and the first of four mechanical signalling outposts on this charming and scenic route appears within half an hour, shortly after departure from New Mills Central. New Mills South Junction is one of those places which remind you of a different era – the start of what was once a section of quadruple line eastwards to Chinley and an outpost of steam activity right up to the end of that era in August 1968.

Today, the four tracks are but a distant memory and the Midland Railway signal box, dating from 1903, now controls the merging of the two routes from Manchester – the route via Romiley used by the stopping services and the route via Stockport used by East Midlands Trains and Trans-Pennine Express services. It is a fairly strenuous but interesting 25-minute walk here from New Mills Central – up to the town centre, down Union Road and crossing an 1884-vintage viaduct over the River Goyt, left and up Church Road for a quarter of a mile then right at Marsh Lane and continuing on for a good half mile or so.

From the Marsh Lane over-bridge there is a good view of the box and junction, but the only semaphore to be seen is an up signal with shunting arm on the Romiley route, that would presumably have been the start of the up slow line. Looking east from the bridge, there is another arm

Barely a mile from Furness Vale, but on an entirely different route (Hope Valley) stands New Mills South Junction, seen here on 29 July 2017 as a TPE Class 185 unit passes the box with a Manchester Airport-Cleethorpes working.

protecting exit from this line onto the main route, alongside an up (eastbound) starter. In the down direction, the home signal is a colour light, with feather lights for access to the Romiley line.

Edale

Returning to New Mills Central and continuing towards Sheffield for another 15 minutes brings you to Edale, a delightful spot that is hugely popular with walkers setting out to tackle Kinder Scout, the 2,088ft peak overlooking this remote station, or join the nearby Pennine Way. The 1893 Midland Railway signal box here stands on the north side of the line, 100 yards west of the station.

Four of its five semaphores can be seen from the station platforms, the missing one being the up home, which stands obscured by a bridge some distance west of the station and box. To the east of the station stand the down home and slightly further out the up starter. Looking back towards Manchester, the down starter stands on a bracket at a point where a goods siding has recently been disconnected, while further out the advanced starter can be seen in the distance from the western end of the up platform (2).

Little more than five minutes after leaving Edale, the train speeds past a third semaphore signalled location at Earle's Sidings, just a short distance west of Hope station and home to a large number of cement wagons. These stand in sidings on

EMT 158889/783 approach Edale on 29 July 2017 with a service from Liverpool Lime Street to Norwich and a backdrop of the Pennines with the two-mile long Cowburn Tunnel visible in the distance.

the south side of the line opposite the 1929 Midland Railway signal box. I noted two semaphores in the up direction and more on the down line, with further signals controlling exit from the sidings complex.

Grindleford

Last of the four mechanically signalled locations on the Hope Valley route is Grindleford, another charming spot that is also a major walking centre and standing at the western end of Totley Tunnel, at 6,230 yards (3½ miles) in length, one of Britain's longest. Here, the most modern of the four boxes, an LMS design from 1938, stands on the south side of the line round a curve some 300 yards west of the station.

Its three semaphores comprise an up starter, with white painted sighting square on a stone bridge behind, while in the down direction, a home signal stands just beyond the platform end and a starter – out of view from the station – stands in front of a bridge carrying a footpath that can be reached with a half mile walk along a track leading to the left as you leave the station.

Northern Rail 142058 has just left Grindleford on 29 July 2017 and passed the 1938 LMS signal box while forming the 12.29 stopping service to Manchester Piccadilly.

CHAPTER 8

SCOTLAND

Scotland has a particularly rich history of railway signalling and the country boasts a significant number of fine signal boxes, many of which remain in use, but many of which have long since ceased to operate. On the West Highland Lines to Oban and Mallaig, for example, which was converted to radio signalling (RETB) in 1987/8, there are no less than ten listed, and now redundant boxes, a number being a distinctive North British Railways (NBR) design and standing on the island platforms that are a feature of this route.

At the time of a review by Historic Scotland and Network Rail of surviving Scottish signal boxes in 2013/4, there were around 150 surviving boxes, some of which were on preserved lines. Of that total, 41 are listed structures, and besides the West Highland, examples include structures ranging from the LNER-built 1936-vintage box just west of Edinburgh Waverley station to the small and apparently ruined wooden box at Elgin Centre, which stands in front of the former Elgin East station, as mentioned below.

Turning to those that are still operational, 16 of Scotland's listed boxes remain in use at the time of writing, although some of these, like Stirling Middle, no longer control any semaphore signals, while those at Nairn and Pitlochry will have joined the list of redundant boxes by the time these words are published. Nevertheless, there is a great deal still to appreciate in Scotland's signalling scene beyond the listed boxes, and there seems no better way of doing it than embarking on what I have called a Grand Highland Tour.

This trip takes us from Edinburgh and follows the Highland Main Line up to Aviemore, the northern extent of manual signalling on that route, then leads us east from the Highland capital of Inverness along the fascinating 108-mile route to Aberdeen, before exploring some of the most notable manual signalling locations on the East Coast route south from Aberdeen towards Dundee and then continuing southwards in the Edinburgh direction.

Falkirk-Grangemouth

Taking a quick detour, the closest of all working mechanical signal boxes to the Scottish capital is Fouldubs Junction, a large and impressive signal box on the freight-only branch from Falkirk to Grangemouth. Getting there is surprisingly easy, with bus routes 3/4/4A to Grangemouth all serving a stop on a large roundabout close to Falkirk Grahamston station and taking you over the line and signal box to a stop called Fouldubs Corner in about 10 minutes (buses about every 15 minutes).

Fouldubs Junction is a large and attractive Caledonian Railway signal box dating from 1908 which controls access to the port and oil refinery at Grangemouth on a freight-only line from Falkirk Grahamston.

A fine collection of semaphore signals at Stirling has all but disappeared in recent years. One of the final two to survive until electrification in late 2018 was the down home (SN36) close to Stirling North Signal Box, seen here on 1 October 2016 as ScotRail 170471 passes with the 09.25 departure for Dunblane.

The signal box stands between the bridge carrying the A905 Beancross Road (along which the bus travels) and another one carrying the M9 motorway. Immediately to the north of the A905 bridge are a number of semaphore controlled sidings, although these are partially obscured by trees and the parapet of the bridge is too high to look over, unless equipped with a stepladder.

Stirling–Perth

Researching the locations and replacement plans for mechanical signalling north of the border, I had noted that the two historic boxes at Stirling, along with those nearby at Larbert North and Dunblane were scheduled for replacement in 2016, so became a priority in planning a visit to the Highland Main Line. I recalled having photographed the delightful array of early semaphores at the south end of Stirling

station in 2009, when I had been taking a first ever trip on the recently re-opened Alloa line, so was hopeful that they would still be there six years later. Both signal boxes at Stirling enjoy a Category A listing, denoting buildings of national or international importance.

Alas, while the historic Stirling Middle signal box remains, all mechanical signalling at the south end of the station had been swept away and replaced by the rather unappealing single aspect colour light signals that are now replacing earlier two, three and four aspect colour lights across the network. Before reaching Stirling on a trip up the Highland Line to Aviemore in September 2016, I noted that the semaphores had already disappeared at Larbert North, although here, too, the signal box remained in use.

The guard on my northbound train from Edinburgh had helpfully told me that the only remaining semaphore at Stirling

was the home signal at the north end of platform 2, just south of the station's other historic signal box, Stirling North. There is, incidentally, a reminder of what this box once controlled at the National Museum of Scotland in Edinburgh, where close to the entrance stand junction signals SN18 and SN11, which were replaced in 2008 when the Alloa line re-opened to passenger traffic. So after a brief interlude to photograph my train passing signal and box – and later spotting a second semaphore, a down starter on the route towards Perth – I continued on to Dunblane in the hope that I was not too late in getting there.

South of the station is controlled by colour light signals, but to the north of the station – where the signal box stands just behind a road bridge – the semaphores remain and at the time of my visit a good place to view the many services from Glasgow and Edinburgh which terminate at the station, then pull forward past the signals and signal box, before crossing to the up line for their return journey.

Continuing north up the Highland Main Line, and on a separate visit (by car) in rather less favourable weather conditions, I was able to visit the four remaining boxes between Stirling and Perth, first of which was at Greenloaning, site of one of just three remaining co-acting semaphore signals on Network Rail (the others being at Cantley and Helsby).

Greenloaning is a small village just off the A9 a few miles north-east of Dunblane. The road into the village crosses the line at the site of a former station and the signal box stands some 300 yards east of the bridge on the south side of the railway line. The co-acting signal (GL27) is what would have been the up starter and is just west of the road bridge, with some telephone wires unhelpfully running in front of it.

Besides this rare feature, it is interesting to note that the home signals in each direction still have shunting arms for loops on either side of the line that have now been disconnected. There are good views to be had from the road bridge in each

Mechanical signalling at the north end of Dunblane station on 1 October 2016 as Virgin Trains East Coast 43367/305 speed past the signal box with the up *Highland Chieftain* service from Inverness to London King's Cross.

One of only three remaining co-acting signals on the national network is GL27, the up starter at Greenloaning, a long-closed (June 1956) station between Stirling and Perth. On 8 December 2016, ScotRail 170413 speeds past with a service for Glasgow Queen Street.

direction, but particularly looking north east towards the signal box and the hills beyond. For a rear shot of up (southbound) trains passing GL27, take a path alongside the River Allan opposite the old station approach and walk around a modern housing development to find a reasonable vantage point close to the line.

Four miles north-east of Greenloaning and once again just north of the A9 is the village of Blackford, home of the Tullibardine distillery and Highland Spring mineral water. The interesting signal box here (LMS, 1933) is at a level crossing to the north side of the village, close to the Highland Spring plant. There is a reasonable vantage point on the south (village) side of the level crossing to photograph trains passing the lattice post down home signal. Looking in the opposite direction, the line passes open country before a down starter signal just in front of a bridge carrying the A9 over the railway.

Despite being some distance from the village it is named after, Auchterarder signal box is very easy to find from the large village, close to Gleneagles. Despite having closed in June 1956, there are prominent signs on the main street to 'Auchterarder station' with no indication that the rail service has long since ceased, and that the site is now a small industrial estate!

It is a mile or so from the village and the best views for photography are to be had from a farm track over-bridge to the south west of the former station site, where the signal box stands on the south side of the line at what would have been the north east end of the up platform. There is a crossover between the two tracks and the remains of a siding on the north (down) side of the line, with three semaphores in view – a home (AR5) and a starter on the down (northbound) side and a home signal on the up side – this and the tall down starter both being lattice posts.

ScotRail 170418 approaches Blackford, another station closed in June 1956, on 8 December 2016, with the 10.10 Glasgow Queen Street-Perth.

A third station between Stirling and Perth to have closed in June 1956 was Auchterarder, close to the famous Gleneagles hotel and golf course. On 8 December 2016, ScotRail 170413 passes the former station site with a Glasgow Queen Street-Aberdeen service.

A fourth surviving mechanical box between Stirling and Perth is at Hilton Junction, where the Ladybank line joins the route from Stirling some way south of Perth. There is a great vantage point to see Hilton Junction signal box – standing between the Ladybank line to the left and the route to Stirling diverging to the right, from a spot on a quiet road leading to the hamlet of Craigend off the A912 road close to where it passes the M90 motorway. Here, you can look down from above the south portal of Moncrieffe Tunnel onto the junction and the gantry above it where HJ6 controls access to the Ladybank line and HJ3 signals the Stirling route. Another semaphore is visible immediately in front of the signal box, controlling northbound exit from the Ladybank line.

Perth-Aviemore

North of Perth, the first sighting of semaphores comes at remote Stanley Junction, where the former Caledonian Railway route to Aberdeen via Forfar once diverged from the Highland Main Line. Since final closure to freight traffic in 1982, this relatively modern British Rail built box, dating from only 1961, has remained operational to control the end of the double track route from Perth and the start of the predominantly single track main line onwards to Inverness.

Stanley has three semaphore arms, the pick of this trio being SJ41, a tall up home signal on a lattice post 300 yards north of the signal box. The other two are down home signals at the end of the double track, with SJ15 on the down (northbound) line being in regular use, but alongside it, SJ16 is only required in the event of wrong line working from Perth, so must seldom see any use. They are easily photographed from a bridge carrying Mill Street, but SJ41 is more of a challenge. It can, however, be seen by walking out of town on Linn Road for about ¾ mile, then taking a path to the left and walking up the side of a ploughed

field to a spot alongside the line, with a good view of the signal and line sweeping round to the signal box.

Having left Stanley Junction behind, the first signal box of note is at Dunkeld, or Dunkeld and Birnham to give its full name, a Grade B Highland Railway structure dating from 1919, which stands at the south end of the down (northbound) platform, opposite the impressive up home signal (DK3), another of the Highland Railway lattice posts that are a delightful feature of this highly scenic main line. Pausing here to await the passing of a late running southbound train offered the opportunity not only to sustain a fall onto the platform, having not spotted the moveable wooden steps that line it, but also to get a great shot of the southbound service approaching the station and passing the two semaphores at the north end of the platforms.

My next port of call was the famous knitting town of Pitlochry, an important stop and passing place. This is the second of four listed boxes on the route from Perth to Inverness, with the Highland Railway box here dating from 1911 and standing at the north end of the down (northbound) platform. The station footbridge provides an excellent vantage point to photograph northbound trains leaving and passing one of the tall Highland Railway lattice post signals that is the down starter (PY21). Looking south, there is a good view of the line and station loop, and a chance to photograph trains crossing, before boarding the northbound service for another leg in the journey towards Aviemore.

A lunchtime break at Blair Atholl meant time to visit the excellent Atholl Arms, next to the station, and a chance to photograph a departing northbound service as it travelled along the double track stretch of route that extends from here to Dalwhinnie, but also to photograph the attractive signal box, which controls a level crossing at the south end of the station as well as the up (southbound)

Stanley Junction ceased to be a junction when the route to Forfar finally closed to freight traffic in 1982, but it still controls the end of double track on the Highland Main Line from Perth. On 17 May 2017, ScotRail 170406 approaches the signal box with the 10.10 Glasgow Queen Street-Inverness.

Dunkeld is one of numerous photogenic spots on the Highland Main Line, with a listed 1919 Highland Railway signal box at the south end of the station. On 1 October 2016, ScotRail 170430 nears the station with the delayed 09.41 Inverness-Edinburgh Waverley.

Another celebrated box along the Highland Main Line is Pitlochry, built by the Highland Railway in 1911. Here 158733 passes the box on 1 October 2016 with the 10.45 Inverness-Edinburgh Waverley.

home signal (BA7), another of the historic lattice posts. By an even greater stroke of luck, not only was the sun shining on the day of my visit, but I was also able to photograph the oil tank train from Lairg on the North Highland Line (a working that has since ceased), as it waited to cross my next northbound service.

On then towards Aviemore, with further signal boxes and semaphores in view at both Dalwhinnie and Kingussie, where a stop on my return trip the following day gave a chance to photograph the HST-formed *Highland Chieftain* as it resumed its 582-mile journey southwards from Inverness to London King's Cross. Kingussie is an important stop on the Highland route, and on weekday mornings

the first 'commuter' stop by the overnight *Caledonian Sleeper* service from London Euston, which picks up early morning travellers heading towards Inverness. The signal box here – situated at the north end of the little used up platform – is an interesting structure which was extended in the 1920s, and which controls a level crossing, as well as the semaphore signalling at both ends of the station.

Aviemore, capital of the Highlands, represents a last outpost of semaphore signalling on the Highland Main Line. Here there is a chance to see steam alongside diesel as the Speyside Railway serves platform three of the historic and listed main station. As at Dalwhinnie, the signal box here is difficult to photograph

Blair Atholl stands at the end of the single track section from Stanley Junction and start of a double-track section north to Dalwhinnie. On 1 October 2016, DB-owned 66111 waits with its train of oil tanks from Lairg on the Far North Line as 170413 comes off the single line with the 12.09 Glasgow Queen Street-Inverness.

Only another 536 miles to King's Cross! The *Highland Chieftain,* formed of Virgin Trains East Coast HST power cars 43307/311, pulls out of the loop at Kingussie on 2 October 2016, on its eight-hour journey from Inverness to London

Steam meets diesel at Aviemore on 2 October 2016, where Strathspey Railway Ivatt 2MT 46512 waits with the 10.30 to Broomhill as Virgin Trains East Coast HST 43307/311 approaches with the up *Highland Chieftain* to London King's Cross.

from the station, being some 300 yards north, and obscured by a huge cellular phone mast. Close to it is the down home signal, while some way to the south end of the station are a pair of up starting signals; like nearby Kingussie, the station is signalled for bi-directional running, so that all trains use the main (down/northbound) platform unless passing another service.

Inverness-Aberdeen

While the Inverness to Aberdeen line may lack the scenic splendour of the North Highland and West Highland lines, it is nevertheless a very pleasant rural route, passing a handful of attractive towns and doing good business. Besides its handful of mechanical signalling outposts, there are a number of well-preserved closed stations as well as distilleries to spot – Glentaucher between Huntly and Keith, Chivas Regal at Keith and Ardmore at Kennethmont. Another rarity and a reminder of past times is the line of seemingly intact telegraph posts and wires on the east side of the line between Insch and Kennethmont.

As mentioned below, a four-year, £170 million investment programme will see capacity on the line improved on its two commuter sections from Inverness to Elgin and Inverurie to Aberdeen, with new signalling, a new station at Forres, double-track from Inverurie south to Aberdeen and preparatory work for two planned new stations, at Dalcross near Inverness, and at Kintore between Inverurie and Dyce. What it has already seen, however, is the elimination of mechanical signalling at Forres and Elgin, with more re-signalling to follow.

Heading back to the south along the 108-mile long Inverness to Aberdeen line, the first sight of mechanical signalling at the time of a visit in March 2017, was at Forres. This is the second station along the route and 24¾ miles east of Inverness. What was once an important triangular junction had long since been reduced to a single curving platform, with a passing loop and signal box some 300 yards north-east of the station.

Trains would pause alongside the signal box to exchange single line tokens for the sections from Nairn to here and onwards

Construction work on a new station and bridge is in evidence behind the two semaphore signals at Forres on 6 March 2017, as ScotRail 158716 passes the signal box with an Aberdeen-bound service.

to Elgin. Signalling at Forres – all to the east side of the station – comprised, in sequence, an up home (FS6), a down home signal (FS21), an up starter (FS7) and a down outer home signal (FS22), which also had a small junction arm (FS18) controlling entry to long redundant sidings north of the old station. One final arm (FS14) controlled exit from these sidings.

But by the time this book is published, all will have been swept away as part of the upgrade. This project, due to be completed in 2019, has now led to a straightening of the rail alignment at Forres, with a new two platform station built to the north of the original Grade II listed building, with elimination of the existing signal box and semaphores. Work at Forres was due to be completed some six months after my visit (it was duly completed in October 2017) and already significant earthworks were taking place in preparation for construction of the new station.

First stop after the new Forres station is Elgin, a place full of railway interest and where its working signal box (at the time of my visit) – Elgin West – stood some 400 yards west of the modern (1990) station and could claim, at that time, to be the most northerly manual signal box in Great Britain. Trains paused here to give up the token from Forres before proceeding into the station. Semaphore interest comprised an up home signal close to the signal box and level crossing (EL17) with down home signals EL4 (platform 1) and EL6 (platform 2).

The up starter signal was already a colour light, but there was a semaphore junction signal on the eastern approach to the station passing loop, not far from the remains of the listed Elgin Centre signal box. This stands at a fork between the Aberdeen route and a former line to Lossiemouth, which closed in 1964, the stub of which remains used for freight traffic. One other feature of the station

area is the magnificent former Elgin East station building, now used as offices, but a reminder of how important railways were in the development of this area.

Keith is a modern single platform station that was once known as Keith Junction and still has the air of grander times past. A bay platform remains signalled and useable, although fenced off. This will hopefully one day see use again if preservationists from the Keith and Dufftown Railway have their way and are able to run trains from here to the famous distillery town.

By comparison with other stations along this route, there are a considerable number of semaphore arms surviving here – all of which are to the east of the station and controlled by Keith Junction signal box, which stands on the north side of the line some 200 yards east of the station and facing the Chivas Regal distillery, once a source of rail freight traffic and the reason

why a number of sidings survive. Close to the 1905-vintage GNS box is a bracket on which are a pair of home signals, with KJ38 for the up main and KJ34 for the passing loop, while exit from the Dufftown platform is controlled by KJ35.

Taking a brisk 15 minute walk past the distillery to an over-bridge on the B9116 road, it is possible to see all of the remaining signals. Looking back towards the station, KJ21 protects a siding alongside the distillery while immediately on the other side of the bridge is a two-arm bracket with KJ8 controlling exit by down trains from the passing loop and KJ11 being a junction arm for the Dufftown platform. Looking further afield towards a large Chivas storage depot there is a pair of up starters at the eastbound exit to the loop and beyond them an outer home another two-signal bracket controlling entry to the loop.

ScotRail 170434 passes Keith Junction Signal Box on 6 March 2017 with the 15.30 departure for Aberdeen. Signal KJ35 to the right protects a platform serving the route to Dufftown.

ScotRail 158712 leaves the bi-directionally signalled passing loop at Huntly on 6 March 2017 with the 12.50 departure for Inverness.

Like Forres, Huntly is a charming and sleepy town with a station on its edge – in this case, though, a very modern structure. The station layout here is a loop around half a mile long which ends just north of the platforms but continues south alongside a number of heavily overgrown sidings east of the line to the signal box and end of the loop.

Signals to the north can easily be photographed from the station footbridge and comprise down starters HT21 (platform 1) and HT23 (platform 2) with a bracket holding a pair of up home signals beyond. South of the station the up home signals are some considerable distance away just in front of the signal box, with another pair of home signals in the down (northbound) direction just beyond the start of the loop.

Insch is a delightful spot, just 27½ miles from Aberdeen and at the southern end of the line's only remaining section of double track, which extends 5½ miles north from here to Kennethmont signal box, the only box on this line not reachable

by the rail-borne traveller. A GNS signal box dating from about 1886 stands at the northern end of the up platform (2) close to a charming station building whose former ticket hall has become the Insch Connection Museum, which features local history and an historic model of the station in the days when it had numerous sidings for the shipping of agricultural products.

Today, the only remaining siding is at the south end of the down platform (1) where it is protected by disc signal IH10. Three other semaphore arms are visible from the station and easily photographed from the station footbridge. To the south, these are an up starter (IH14) and a down home signal (IH2) while north of the station and level crossing, where the line curves to the left, there is an up home signal with a down starter (IH3) further round the curve and out of sight of the station.

The final manual signals on this route – sadly, the listed box at nearby Dyce only has colour lights – are at Inverurie. This once important railway town boasted a major locomotive works, but all that

ScotRail 170428 nears the end of a short section of double track from Kennethmont and arrives at Insch on 6 March 2017, with the 12.35 to Aberdeen. Note the rare sight of telegraph poles and wires to the right of the line.

ScotRail 170433 departs Inverurie on 5 March 2017 with the 14.58 to Aberdeen. The section of line from here to the Granite City is due to be re-doubled as part of a £170m upgrading of the Inverness-Aberdeen route.

remain are a few rusted sidings to the north of the station. Today it remains a significant station however, with many Class 170-worked services from Glasgow and Edinburgh terminating here and supplementing the two-hourly Inverness to Aberdeen services to give a commuter frequency on the soon-to-be-doubled section of line south to Aberdeen.

Signalling here is controlled from a GNS box dating from 1902 which stands some way back from the line to the north of the up platform (2). This platform only sees a handful of trains each day, with most using the main down platform (1). Signalling here to the south comprises up starters IE26 (platform 2) and IE28 (platform 1) with junction down home signals beyond on a two arm bracket. An identical pattern of signals controls the northern end of the station.

Virgin Trains East Coast HST, comprising power cars 43257/272, pulls out of Stonehaven on 7 March 2017 with the delayed 12.41 departure for Aberdeen.

Aberdeen-Dundee

Heading south from the granite city, one of the finest signal boxes still operating semaphore signals can be found at Stonehaven. Here there is a Listed Caledonian Railway Type 2 box, dating in its present form from 1901, but the extension of a much earlier Caledonian Railway box dating from the opening of the station in 1849. It stands at the northern end of the southbound (up) platform 2 and seems to control a total of six semaphore arms, with three at each end of the station.

To the north, a down home (SV17) stands at the end of platform 1, while 100 yards beyond is a tall lattice post holding the up home signal. Further away, around a left hand bend, is an advanced down starter. To the south of the station, the up starter (SV8) is another shorter

lattice post, beyond which are a down outer home and an up advanced starter, all clearly visible from the platform end. Like the signal box, the unusual two-storey Stonehaven station, which was restored in 2000, is also Listed.

Continuing south and passing more semaphore survivors at Carmont, Craigo and Laurencekirk, the next significant station with any remaining mechanical arms is Montrose. Re-signalling south of here in 2010 meant the end of mechanical signals and boxes at Montrose South and Usan – incidentally the only section of single track between Aberdeen and London – but the listed 1881 box at Montrose North survived, albeit with just three remaining semaphores, being recommissioned after a four-year closure. Its working semaphores include a pair of down (northbound) home signals standing 200 yards north of the station immediately in front of the box itself, where there is a crossover between the two tracks. This allows northbound services to use the up platform (1),

which is long enough for a full length 9-coach HST.

Travelling south for another 15 minutes, passing another isolated box with semaphores at Inverkeilor, brings you to the splendid 1911 station at Arbroath and what must be the finest surviving box on the line, Arbroath North. This magnificent survival can easily be seen from the platform ends but can be viewed at close quarters only a short walk from the station at the level crossing it controls. From here it is worth going through the car park of a large Morrisons superstore to a bridge over the line on the A933 road.

Unlike the station building, which was not considered worthy of listing, Arbroath North signal box has a number of unique features, as cited in the reasons for its listing in the Scottish Signal Box Review (2012-13). This is a variation on what is known as a North British Railway (NBR) Type 7 box, which was designed specifically for its location, where additional height was required to obtain good views of the rail traffic.

ScotRail 170413 passes Montrose North Signal Box on 7 March 2017 with the 14.10 departure for Aberdeen and Inverurie.

A view looking north from the A9133 road bridge at Arbroath as ScotRail 170453 accelerates away with the 14.54 departure for Aberdeen.

The citation goes on to point out that, 'It is the only signal box in the country with an oversailing signal cabin supported on metal brackets projecting toward the track. The prominent location beside a level crossing and its and group value with the adjacent cast-iron pedestrian bridge add to the interest.'

A thankfully low parapet to the A933 bridge gives an interrupted view north where you can see the down starter (AH45) – another lattice post – alongside a tall up home signal AH15 with a small shunting arm (AH19) alongside it. Venture another 300 yards up a residential street called Ogilvy Place and you come to another footbridge (there is also one adjacent to the signal box). Here you get a great view of the up home and the lines heading into the station while looking north beyond the end of a redundant siding there is an up outer home signal. Back at the station,

and similar to Stonehaven, the up starter AH16 is another short lattice post, with the other station signal being down home (AH47)

Dundee-Perth

Before heading over the Tay Bridge and discovering two final outposts of semaphore signalling on our final leg of the Grand Highland Tour back to Edinburgh, it is well worth making a slight diversion along the north bank of the River Tay, where the route back to Stirling – as travelled by Glasgow-Aberdeen services – features three interesting and attractive signal boxes, one of which features in the schedule of Listed boxes. For those like me without their own wheels, they can all be visited (with a bit of walking involved) by catching the hourly Stagecoach bus 16 from Dundee to Perth.

Almost eight miles south-west of Dundee and around 35 minutes on the 16 bus, the first of this surviving trio of manual signal boxes stands a mile south of Longforgan village and at the site of a long closed (June 1956) station. Here there is an LMS box dating from 1929, very similar in style to the one at Blackford, which controls level crossing barriers and has two remaining semaphores. These are both in the down (northbound) direction, with one (LF2) just 100 yards west of the box and a second (LF4) some 400 yards back along the line towards Dundee.

Returning to Longforgan village and carrying on for another six miles aboard the 16 bus, brings you to a turn for a hamlet called Errol Station, about a mile north-east of Errol. The Listed Caledonian Railway signal box here dates from 1877 and stands just west of the remarkably well-preserved station. This only closed in 1985 and both platforms remain intact along with the skeleton of an iron footbridge, while the privately-owned main station building on the down (northbound) side has a plaque on

it with the date 1847. Errol box controls six semaphores – three in each direction – with the finest being the lattice posted up home (ER9). The best vantage point here is up a lane passing south of the old station, where there is a fine view of the box, station and two tall semaphores, down starter ER15 and up outer home ER8.

Finally, just a mile before Perth and on the east bank of the River Tay stands Barnhill signal box. This controls access to the section of single track over the curving Tay Viaduct leading to a straight section of line that passes the platform of the former Princes Street station and on to the main railway station. There is a footpath alongside the railway track on the Tay Viaduct, from which it is possible to see the box and two semaphores – a tall lattice post in the up direction (BH16) and a down home just after the Viaduct (BH2). For a good view of the signal box, walk down Island View, a short cul-de-sac leading off Dundee Road, where it is also possible to see – though not photograph – two further semaphore arms on the double track looking back towards Dundee.

ScotRail 170404 approaches the signal box and level crossing at Longforgan on 16 May 2017, while working the 11.41 Glasgow Queen Street-Aberdeen.

With grey skies overhead and a shower looming, ScotRail 170456 speeds through the closed station at Errol on 16 May 2017 with the 13.41 Glasgow Queen Street-Aberdeen.

ScotRail 170431 passes Barnhill Signal Box, just east of Perth, on 16 May 2017 and is about to go onto the single-track Tay Viaduct, with the 15.33 Aberdeen-Glasgow Queen Street.

South from Dundee

Back to the main line, little more than ten minutes after leaving Dundee and passing over the impressive Tay Bridge brings you to the busy island platform at Leuchars, a station linked to nearby St. Andrews by a seemingly endless succession of buses pulling up outside the station. Here, four semaphore arms are visible from the station – LE20 (down home), LE29 (up starter) – with down starter and up home visible from the north end of the station, where the signal box stands on the east side of the line. Good vantage points for photos are from the station footbridge (looking north towards signal box and left-hand curve) and from a road bridge south of the station where there is a good view of the station and its substantial island platform.

One final outpost of manual signalling on our journey back to Edinburgh is at Cupar, just seven rail minutes south from Leuchars. Here there are three semaphore arms, an up home (not visible from the station), an up starter, and a down starter north of the signal box on the west side of the line. The attractive and historic station building, standing on the down (town) side of the station, is now partly used as a museum with space for a relief line between the two platform lines.

Virgin Trains East Coast HST, comprising power cars 43238/208, passes Leuchars Signal Box and is about to call at Leuchars station on 7 December 2016 with the *Northern Lights* service from Aberdeen to London King's Cross.

South-west of Glasgow - towards Carlisle

Away from the Highlands, remaining semaphore interest in Scotland lies principally on two routes leading south from Glasgow. These are the southern end of the route via Ayr to Stranraer Harbour and the former Glasgow & South Western (GSW) route via Kilmarnock and Dumfries to Carlisle. Taking a trip on the GSW route to visit the only two boxes located at stations, the first sight of semaphores comes at Lugton, just 13½ miles south of Glasgow, where an impressive LMS box dating from 1929 stands on the west side of the line and controls access to the section of single track north from here to Barrhead.

Continuing on through Kilmarnock, there is a fine array of semaphore arms at Mauchline, junction for a freight route westwards. Then, shortly after another junction, this time to two open cast sites at Greenburn and Knockshinnoch, we come to the remote station at New Cumnock. Sadly gone now is its co-acting signal, a former

up advanced starter now a colour light, with remaining interest being an up starter (NC31) at the end of platform 2, a tall down starter beyond the signal box at the north end of platform 1 and an up home signal some way beyond, with a small Junction arm controlling access to a loop and sidings to the east of the station. Also worthy of note are two shunting disc signals mounted on a short lattice post under the road bridge and adjacent to the up platform.

Just over seven miles – or nine minutes by train – brings you to Kirkconnel, the other station on this route with a signal box and semaphores. The box here is some distance north of the station and controls four semaphore arms – including an up advanced starter (KC11) at the south end of the station, a down or northbound home signal (KC40) and an up starter standing close to the signal box. A footbridge midway along the platforms gives a good vantage point for taking photos. Like New Cumnock, the station is unstaffed but lacks the historic (albeit locked) station building which survives at New Cumnock.

One of the few remaining flows of coal traffic in the UK is from open cast mining activities in Ayrshire. On 8 March 2017, GBRf 66750 nears the end of its journey as it passes New Cumnock with a train of empty wagons from Tyne Coal Terminal heading for the nearby Greenburn open cast mine.

Kirkconnel is a pleasant and quiet spot on the Glasgow & South Western (GSW) Route. On 8 March 2017, ScotRail 156435 departs with the 13.24 service to Carlisle.

Thornhill is a remarkably well-preserved station (closed December 1965) on the GSW route, which has been identified for possible re-opening. On 26 April 2017, 156501 passes with the 10.13 Glasgow Central-Carlisle.

One final outpost of mechanical signalling on the GSW route is at Holywood, a few miles north west of Dumfries. On 26 April 2017, ScotRail 156501 passes the signal box and former station (closed September 1949) with the 13.12 Carlisle-Glasgow Central.

Heading on towards Dumfries, the penultimate manual box on the Glasgow and South Western route is at Thornhill, a sizeable settlement which lost its station in December 1965, but is a potential re-opening candidate, although possibly at a site closer to the town than the former station, which is over a mile north-east of the main street. Thornhill is a war-time box dating from 1943, which was actually closed for a number of years before being reopened to handle increased traffic on the line and stands 200 yards south of the remarkably intact platforms of the former station. To the south end of the up side former platform, the only signals to be seen are an up home on a tall lattice post (TH8) alongside which is a shorter and newer arm (TH10), controlling access to an up goods loop. There are also a couple of shunting discs alongside the down line to control a trailing crossover in front of the box.

Finally on this route, Scotland's most southerly mechanical signal box stands at Holywood, four miles north of Dumfries, where a G&SWR box dating from 1920 controls mechanically-worked wooden gates on a quiet country lane around a mile from the village. Curiously Holywood station is signposted off the A76 trunk road, despite having closed to passengers as long ago as September 1949. Four semaphore arms are visible at the crossing – a tall home and shorter starter in the down direction, an outer up home beyond a road bridge to the north and a short home signal in the up direction close to the box. For the best vantage point, it is worth heading for a farm crossing over-bridge, half a mile south of the crossing.

South-west of Glasgow - to Stranraer Harbour

Leaving the GSW line at Kilmarnock and heading across to the Ayr and the Ayrshire coast, the most fascinating of all mechanical signalling outposts in Scotland can be found on the stretch of line south of Ayr and on towards Stranraer Harbour, where there are six remaining manual boxes, although the one at Stranraer Harbour has been 'switched out' since November 2007 and is now only opened occasionally for the occasional special traffic on the line. What makes this route so interesting from a signalling point of view is that it is the last route in Great Britain to be controlled, in part at least, by Electric Train Tablet, using large round discs which are inserted and removed from machines in the boxes at Barrhill, Glenwhilly and Dunragit called a Tyer's No. 6 instrument.

Beginning a journey down this very scenic line, the first mechanical signalling interest comes around ten minutes after leaving the station at Maybole, where the double line becomes single at Kilkerran. At this remote spot, the long- closed (September 1965) station building still stands next to the quiet level crossing controlled by the first of the six surviving manual boxes on the Stranraer route. The 1895 box here controls a handful of semaphore arms, most of which are visible from the level crossing, but, unlike boxes further south, the Tokenless Block applying to the route as far as Girvan means that there is no exchanging of tokens here for the single line from here to Girvan.

Ten miles beyond Kilkerran the line reaches its major intermediate station at Girvan. It has long been popular as a leisure destination for Glaswegians, with a fine beach and the amazing sight of Ailsa Craig, a large rocky outcrop standing almost ten miles offshore and locally known as 'Paddy's Milestone'. The signal box here is one of two listed boxes on the Stranraer route, a GSW Type 3 box from 1893, which shares its listing with the adjacent station building.

From a signalling viewpoint, the only photo opportunity at the station is to look south where there are down starters just beyond both platform ends, with the up home (GV27) visible at the end of the passing loop. There are no signals to be seen looking north, where the line curves to the right and crosses the Water

Scotrail 156478 approaches Kilkerran Signal Box and the site of a former station (closed September 1965) while working the 13.00 Girvan-Ayr on 25 April 2017.

ScotRail 156478 nears the end of its journey from Ayr on 25 April 2017 as it approaches Girvan. Note the surviving pair of shunting arms to the right of the train.

of Girvan, but take a brisk 15 minute walk out of town along the A77 and then scramble down a bank and you reach an old road bridge over the line. From here, a road leading to Girvan Golf Course offers a good vantage point to see down home signals GV4 and GV6 at the start of the long station passing loop, with a couple of shunting arms protecting a siding to the north end of the loop.

Just under 20 minutes after leaving Girvan, it is time to give up the first of the single line tablets at the Stranraer line's last remaining intermediate station, Barrhill which, with just two parking spaces, must have the smallest advertised car park of any British railway station! Here, a diminutive signal cabin stands on the down platform, controlling the passing loop and four semaphore arms, of which all except the up home signal (BR15) can be seen from the platform. Here the Barrhill signaller exchanges the

Girvan tablet for one covering the section to Glenwhilly.

Scotland's remotest signal box is such a quiet spot that a pair of oyster catchers had built a nest between the tracks at the time of my April 2017 visit, with the female sitting on a clutch of eggs but flying off every time a train passed! Glenwhilly is some 12 miles south of Barrhill and the site of a station that closed in September 1965. Besides remoteness, Glenwhilly's other claim to fame is having the last working distant signal in Scotland among the five semaphores it controls, a down distant (GW1) which can be seen from the narrow road which parallels the line almost a mile north of the box. From the former station site, the remaining signals can all be seen, with a down home (GW3) and up starter (GW19) looking north and down starter GW2 and up home GW18 at the south end of the passing loop just before the line sweeps round to the left.

Barrhill's up starter (BR14) looks badly in need of a new coat of paint as ScotRail 156512 departs the one remaining station between Girvan and Stranraer on 25 April 2017, with the 11.40 to Kilmarnock.

Just off the A75 and controlling a quiet level crossing is the attractive and listed signal box in the village of Dunragit which, like Glenwhilly, lost its station in 1965. This 1927 LMS box is of a Midland Railway design known as Type 12 whose distinguishing feature is the projecting centre bay of the three bay frontage. Today, it is the last working box on the trip to Stranraer, so with the Harbour box normally closed, drivers will surrender the tablet from Glenwhilly here and be given a key token for the section to Stranraer.

There are a total of five semaphores here, which can all be seen from the level crossing – looking back towards Glenwhilly, there are down outer home DR12 and up starter DR25, which are both tall lattice posts, with home signal DR13 close to the signal box, while looking west to a bridge carrying the A75 over the line are down starter DR14 and up home DR27, which stands under the road bridge.

Finally, we reach journey's end some six miles beyond Dunragit at Stranraer, where the Harbour station is a sad reminder of traffic lost, with a desolate walk from the town centre taking you past the huge parking areas formerly used by ferry traffic, but now empty and waiting for possible replacement by a marina. The smart 1897 GSW box here has been switched out for over a decade, being opened only for occasional special traffic.

It means that signals on the line into platform 1 are left in the off position, with deep rust on the line into platform 2 and run round loop suggesting that it is a very long time since they last saw use. How long the layout and signalling here will remain frozen in time is a matter for some speculation, given local talk of truncating the line to open a new terminus close to the former Stranraer Town station.

The Dunragit signaller prepares to take the single line Tyer's Tablet for the section from Glenwhilly from the driver of ScotRail 156442 on 24 April 2017. In return, he will give the driver a Key Token for the section to Stranraer Harbour.

Rusting rails and most signals being permanently in the 'off' position are reminders of how long it is since Stranraer Harbour Signal Box was in regular use to handle the once heavy ferry traffic from Ireland. On 24 April 2017, 156439 departs with the 16.59 to Glasgow Central.

Fort William Junction

More than three decades after the rest of the West Highland lines from Glasgow to Oban and Mallaig were converted to radio signalling (RETB) in 1987/8, one charming reminder of the past is Fort William Junction, just north-east of Fort William station and convergence of the route from Glasgow with the Mallaig extension. Here, a North British Railway box dating from 1894 stands in the fork between the two lines and has nine semaphore arms under its control, along with a handful of disc shunting signals.

There is a good vantage point close to the box from a bridge carrying a path that leads from the A82 road just beyond an oil depot. This path leads to a housing estate north of the Mallaig line and, by following a path on the line-side of the estate, it is possible to reach a second good viewing spot from a footbridge just short of sidings used by West Coast Railways to store the steam locomotives and stock of its 'Jacobite' service to Mallaig.

From the first bridge, a look towards the town reveals the only modern semaphore post in the area, a very tall galvanised steel structure overlooking the oil depot sidings, where the sleeper loco is stored during the day. This has a Junction arm for Mallaig (FW27), a taller signal (FW24) for the main line and a shunting signal beneath. Looking towards the box there is a tall home signal (FW7) protecting exit from the Mallaig line, with a shorter one (FW13) on the approach from Glasgow. Out of sight beyond the A82 road over-bridge in the distance is another up signal near a junction for sidings serving the aluminium smelting works, the only remaining source of regular freight traffic on the route.

Standing on the footbridge close to the two sets of sidings, there is a view back towards the box of Mallaig starter signal FW26, partially obscured by a tree, while looking north and alongside the West Coast Railways sidings are outer home signal FW6 and a section signal in the Mallaig direction (FW25) with a notice on it advising drivers that it marks the start of radio token working.

Fort William Junction is a remarkable survival on a route which was converted to radio signalling (RETB) in 1987/88. On 6 October 2017, 73971 brings the Fort William portion of the *Caledonian Sleeper* past home signal FW13.

CHAPTER 9

IRELAND

In common with Great Britain, Ireland has a master-plan for its railway signalling, in this case one to replace what is known as its Centralised Traffic Control Centre (CTCC), which is situated at Dublin's Connolly station and has controlled 1,500kms (940 miles) or around 75 per cent of the network since its development in the 1970s.

Irish Rail (Iarnród Éireann or IE) invited tenders for its replacement in February 2016, saying that a new system, to be known as NTCC, was necessary due to capacity restraints with the existing CTCC facility. The new centre, to be operational by 2022, will integrate signalling and communications control across the entire 2,400km (1,500 mile) IE network, so should spell a final end to mechanical signalling in the Republic.

Manual signalling has already disappeared from almost all the Irish rail network, with the exception of two little-used cross country lines, both of which have been longstanding candidates for closure, but each hangs on today with sparse services of just two trains each way per day. These are the routes from Waterford to Limerick Junction and from Limerick to Ballybrophy, which share the distinction of being the most poorly performing routes on the entire IE network. In addition to these, there are a couple of other semaphore survivals, as mentioned below.

My interest in Irish railway signalling dates back to a memorable visit made in September 2010 to travel on the very last passenger services between Rosslare Europort and Waterford. Like the two surviving routes with manual signalling, it had long been seen as a candidate for closure, with its one train a day service reputedly carrying only around 30 passengers a day. On top of that, the once important sugar beet traffic from Wellingtonbridge, its principal intermediate station, had ceased a few years before and there were around a dozen manned level crossings along the 30-mile line, to further undermine its economics.

So, setting out from Paddington on the evening of Friday, 17 September 2010, I had taken a nocturnal journey to Fishguard Harbour, slept for about three hours in a lounge on the *Stena Europe* and woken at 05.30 the following morning, before heading off once we docked at 06.30 for the very basic railway station at Rosslare Harbour. Here, a class 2700 unit (vehicles 2726/2723) formed the last ever 07.00 departure for Waterford. We set off on time with about 30 passengers on board, a number which had increased to 48 by the time of our 08.20 arrival at Waterford Plunkett station.

Waterford-Limerick Junction

The final journey back from Waterford was not until 17.20, so faced with an entire day to fill, I decided to extend my knowledge of Irish railways a little further by taking a lunch-time train (since withdrawn) on the 58-mile cross country route to Limerick Junction, not knowing at the time of its particular rarity from a signalling perspective. Before leaving Waterford Plunkett, I did have time (and the good sense, with hindsight) to photograph the fine collection of semaphores at the western approach to the station, which were controlled by the highly impressive Waterford Central signal box, standing on a gantry above the through running lines.

From Waterford, the train made three stops at stations with signal boxes, passing loops and semaphore signals – Carrick-on-Suir, Clonmel and Tipperary – and there was time on this leisurely one hour 42 minute journey to alight at each stop and photograph the token exchange and some of the semaphore signals at each station. Once at Limerick Junction, my mind had been on trying (in vain as it happened) to get a pint of Guinness before the return service at 15.10, but I did at least have the presence of mind to photograph the two signal boxes and the curious mixture of manual and colour light signalling at the north end of the station.

Paying a return visit to the line some six and a half years later (January 2017), there had been a fair amount of change. Firstly, the service itself had been rationalised to just two return journeys a day, with a nine-hour gap between services, which would be enough to put off all but the most intrepid traveller. Irish Railways is very good at marketing bargain online

fares on its principal routes, such as Cork-Dublin and Limerick-Dublin, but funnily enough there are no bargains to be had on this threatened route, so it is hardly surprising perhaps that the service I took – the 09.45 from Limerick Junction – had barely 20 passengers on board by the time it reached its destination.

Secondly, there has been some drastic rationalisation of the layout at Carrick-on-Suir, where the passing loop had recently been removed and only one siding remained, making it slightly curious that it remained as a block post. The re-signalling of Limerick Junction has brought MAS signalling towards Tipperary, but happily, the box and semaphore signalling here remains unchanged, along with wooden level crossing gates, while Clonmel is now the only remaining station with two platforms, although the sparse service means that all services normally use platform 1. What I had missed on my earlier visit was the handful of gate boxes – two of which are at the site of disused stations – which each retain a couple of

The way it was at Carrick-on-Suir before track rationalisation. IE 2726 approaches the station with a Waterford-Limerick Junction service on 18 September 2010.

It's a long, long way to Tipperary! On 17 January 2017, the Tipperary signaller hands over a single-line token for the section to Clonmel to the driver of 22205/305, forming the 09.45 Limerick Junction-Waterford Plunkett.

Despite the loss of signalling at Plunkett station, Waterford West Signal Box survives and controls a few semaphores. These include WT5, which IE 22249/22349 passes with the 10.15 from Dublin Heuston on 17 January 2017.

semaphore signals to protect their level crossings.

What has changed most in the past six years, however, is the rather sad and rationalised scene at Waterford Plunkett. Here, a cliff fall means that the main station platform has now been permanently fenced off, the splendid Waterford Central signal box on a gantry over the through running lines is no longer in use, all the station's semaphore signals have now gone and only one of two bay platforms (platform 5) is now open for use.

Remarkably, Waterford West signal box remains in use for the present, controlling a handful of semaphore signals, as well as some lights, and I was able to get a good shot of the 10.15 from Dublin Heuston passing a two-signal bracket west of the signal box, after a 20-minute walk along the main R448 Newrath Road, which passes immediately to the south of the station and crosses the line just to its west. Steps down to a small industrial estate lead to a level crossing, from where there is a good view of a two-signal

bracket, with Waterford West signal box beyond.

Limerick-Ballybrophy

What must unquestionably rank as the most remarkable rail survivor in Ireland is a 52-mile long backwater that runs north east from Limerick to a junction with the Dublin-Cork main line at Ballybrophy. It is officially the country's worst performing rail route, with a recent government report suggesting that each of the line's 50 or so daily passengers is subsidised to the tune of more than €760 per passenger journey. Yet still it hangs on and, in so doing, remains Ireland's other significant outpost of manual signalling.

Services on the route comprise two return journeys daily, with departures from Limerick Colbert on weekdays at 06.30 and 16.55 and return services from Ballybrophy at 10.05 and 19.05. With a speed limit of 30mph on much of the line, trains are timed to take exactly two hours for the journey, and at Ballybrophy make

good connections into services to and from Dublin. But passengers to and from Limerick are unlikely to be tempted to use this route if heading for the capital, as direct services, or those requiring a change at Limerick Junction, offer a saving of around an hour compared to the journey via Ballybrophy. Consulting the IE online journey planner for an early morning Limerick-Dublin journey does not even show this route as an option.

In addition to the full length journeys on the line, there is also a Monday to Friday only short journey from the principal intermediate station, Nenagh, into Limerick. This unbalanced working is made possible by attaching an extra two-car set to the 06.30 from Limerick, which is then detached at Nenagh in order to form the service (07.45) to Limerick. Like other services I saw or travelled on, the commuter traffic it attracts seems pretty thin – I counted nine passengers alighting when this service arrived at Limerick Colbert on a morning in January 2017.

Taking a trip on the line is a delightful and fairly solitary experience. I was the only passenger aboard the 06.30 departure from Limerick on the first day I travelled the line, and after a handful of joiners at the five intermediate stations, there were a total of eight passengers on board by the time the train reached its destination at Ballybrophy. Returning on the 10.05 service to Limerick Colbert, there seemed few takers for the attractive €6.00 return fare on offer at intermediate stations, with just ten of us (plus a baby) alighting from the train at its destination.

Leaving the Limerick Junction route at Killonan Junction, just over four miles south-east of Limerick, the line takes its north-easterly course, reaching its first intermediate stop at Castleconnell, some 20 minutes after departure from the terminus. This is one of three stations along the route with semaphore signals, in this case though it is just a gate box controlling a level crossing immediately to the north of the single platform, with the northbound signal situated midway along the platform.

Next up is Birdhill, the first of the two block posts along the route, with a lengthy passing loop and attractive signal box.

Dawn is only just breaking at Roscrea on 18 January 2017 and few passengers are waiting as IE 2808 arrives with the 10.27 service to Limerick Colbert.

An interesting signalling feature to note here was that the signaller gave two tokens to the driver of my 06.30 train, one of which was then taken by the driver of the second two-car unit, who would be working the service back to Limerick from Nenagh, the next station along the line. As Nenagh is only halfway along the block section to Roscrea, Birdhill controls a colour light home signal on the northbound approach to Nenagh.

Nenagh is an attractive and staffed station, with a couple of sidings but no passing loop, although a blocked off footbridge remains across to the disused but tidily maintained southbound platform. A boarded up signal cabin stands at the south end of the platform here, as well as at the following station, Cloughjordan.

By far the most attractive station along the line is Roscrea, the final stop before Ballybrophy, with a fine and listed station building and a signal box standing at the east end of the opposite, and disused, platform. There is a goods shed and sidings to the east of the station, which stands to the north of this small town, once home to a large – now disused – pharmaceuticals plant and now dominated an enormous Tesco superstore.

Ballybrophy station sees a rather sparse service of trains on the main Dublin-Cork axis, although good connections are made in and out of the two Nenagh line services, which use a bay platform on the west side of the station. Two features of note at the station are a turntable, which must surely have potential for restoration and use in connection with steam specials, and what looks like a working water column at the south end of the Cork-bound platform, the only such column I spotted in a week touring the area by rail.

Eager to relieve the Irish taxpayer of another €760, I took a second trip from Limerick to Ballybrophy two days after my first foray, and being a Friday there seemed to have been something of an uptick in passengers. Two of us were on board the 06.30 departure from Limerick Colbert (along with four IE staff) and my fellow traveller alighted at Nenagh. Despite no custom at either Castleconnell or Birdhill, both of which had produced passengers on Wednesday, things then picked up. There were four joiners at Nenagh, another four adults and two children at Cloughjordan and an impressive five boarding at Roscrea, making a grand total of fourteen adults and two children on our arrival at Ballybrophy!

A future in doubt

A very dark cloud currently hangs over both the Limerick Junction-Waterford and the Limerick-Ballybrophy lines. This follows publication in August 2016 of a major Rail Review by the National Transport Authority and IE. This confirmed that they were by far the country's poorest performing routes, and suggested that they were candidates for closure, along with the Western Rail Corridor route from Limerick to Galway – which only re-opened fully in 2009 – and the southern end of the Dublin-Rosslare route between Gorey and Rosslare.

Besides confirming the huge cost per passenger of running the Ballybrophy route, it also put another eye-watering figure on the Limerick Junction-Waterford route of €362.40 per passenger journey. Put crudely, that meant that in a four-day visit touring the country on a €110 'Trekker' rover ticket, the three journeys I had taken on the Ballybrophy line and the one along the Waterford line had cost the Irish Government a staggering total of more than €2,500! By comparison to these lines, the financial performance of the other two big loss makers looks relatively modest, with the Western Rail Corridor route reputedly costing the state €44.00 per passenger journey and the Dublin-Rosslare route €29.10.

At a time when overall rail revenues and passenger numbers were on the rise in Ireland, what is particularly alarming about the figures for these two mechanically-signalled routes, is that they alone in Ireland saw the subsidy cost per passenger increase between 2014 and 2015 – in the case of Ballybrophy from €417.20 in 2014 to €551.90 the following year. As in Great Britain, closure of lines arouses great passions, as I had discovered when I met leading lights in the long campaign to save the Waterford-Rosslare route during my journey on the final train in September 2010, so the fate of these two routes may not yet be sealed, but things do look pretty bleak.

That gloomy assessment was repeated a year later on 7 September 2017, when IE's latest annual report painted a generally improving overall picture, with a lower overall operating deficit, but indicated that closure of the Limerick to Ballybrophy and Limerick Junction to Waterford routes could save in excess of €5 million a year, with a further potential saving of €4.4 million from closure of the Gorey to Rosslare route.

Limerick Check

Re-signalling at Limerick Junction had not affected the north-western end of the 21-mile branch to Limerick's Colbert station, which at the time of my January 2017 visit still boasted a signal box, along with two others nearby at Limerick Check, about half a mile from the terminus and at Killonan Junction, just over four miles from Colbert, where the section of double track ends and where the Ballybrophy line diverges.

One solitary semaphore in this area stood close to the Limerick Check box, a two arm post, which appeared to control exit onto the main line from the 'mothballed' 26-mile branch line from Foynes, a major container port on the Shannon, whose owners have talked about re-opening the line to freight traffic. Sadly, I read six months after my January 2017 visit that re-signalling in the Limerick area (June 2017) had meant closure of the Limerick signal boxes.

Cork Kent

When a major resignalling project known as Cork East was completed in 2010, it put an end to mechanical signalling at two locations on the suburban network radiating east from Ireland's second city – at Glounthaune, or Cobh Junction as it was better known, and at the port terminus of Cobh itself. Today, both boxes survive, with the one at Cobh now boarded up and the small box on platform one at Glounthaune still a feature of the station building, with its 20 or so mechanical levers still looking ready for service and even a pair of spectacles left on a desk

in the cabin by one of its last occupants in 2010!

But in a uniquely Irish piece of re-signalling, this was not completely the end of semaphore signalling in the area. The three bay platforms at Cork Kent station used by the services to Midleton and Cobh remained controlled by a trio of mechanical signals, with a bracket hosting signals CK73 and CK74, controlling exit from platforms 1 and 2, while a solitary CK75 signalled trains departing from platform 3. Quite why what are probably the station's most actively used signals (at peak times there are four departures an hour) had remained mechanically worked from the nearby Cork signal box is something of a mystery, and, alas, I read that this trio were all replaced by colour lights in November 2018.

This trio of semaphores seem an unlikely survival at Cork Kent station. Here IE2615/6 departs on 19 January 2017 with the 12.00 to Cobh.

IE 2605/6 arrives at Glounthaune station on 19 January 2017 with a service to Cobh. Despite re-signalling, the small signal cabin, which controlled the busy junction here, remains untouched behind the windows of the station building.

Token exchange at Clonmel on 17 January 2017, as the driver of the 09.45 Limerick Junction – Waterford Plunkett gives up the single token for the section from Tipperary.

BIBLIOGRAPHY

A great deal of scholarly work has been published on all aspects of railway signalling. Below is a brief list of those books and reference sources which I have found invaluable in preparing this work, none more so than the Signalling Record Society's *Signalling Atlas*.

In terms of researching what to expect at the many locations – particularly freight movements – I have relied heavily on www.realtimetrains.co.uk. I have also found many helpful pictures, diagrams and notes in enthusiast forums and on individual websites, notably www.signalbox.org, www.scot-rail.co.uk and www.roscalen.com.

I am deeply indebted to all those whose wisdom I have shamelessly used to direct me to the best signalling locations, and to those signallers and other railwaymen who I have spoken to on my travels, and whose comments and anecdotes have helped further my knowledge and bring this story alive.

ALLEN, David, 'Fylde signalling before electrification', *Rail* magazine issue 828/7-20 June 2017

BURKE, M., *Signalman*, Bradford Barton (publication date unknown)

CONNOR, Piers, *British Signalling – What the driver sees*, PRC Rail Consulting, Railway Technical Website, 7 May 2017

Institution of Railway Signal Engineers *Introduction to Signalling*

KAY, Peter and ALLEN, David, *Signalling Atlas and Signal Box Directory (Third Edition)*, Signalling Record Society, 2010

KESSELL, Clive, 'UK Signalling – A 2017 update' *Rail Engineer*, 23 February 2017

KICHENSIDE, Geoffrey and WILLIAMS, Alan, *Two Centuries of Railway Signalling (Revised Second Edition)*, Oxford Publishing Company, 2016

MINNIS, John, *Railway Signal Boxes – A Review,* English Heritage, 2012

National Transport Authority/Iarnrod Eirann (Irish Rail), *Rail Review 2016 Report* August 2016

RHODES, Michael, *Resignalling Britain*, Mortons Media, 2015

INDEX